Journalist and author for over thirty years, Dublin-born Heather Parsons has worked as both Editor and writer on a number of leading Irish newspapers and magazines. Her career has ranged across a variety of areas, from women's and human interest to news, investigative reports and show business.

In June 1985, she travelled to Medjugorje in what was then communist Yugoslavia to investigate reports of alleged daily apparitions of the Virgin Mary to six children. It was an assignment that was to change her life.

This is her third book on the phenomenon that is Medjugorje.

By the same author

A Light between the Hills
Marija and the Mother of God
Fr. Peter Rookey – Man of Miracles

Heather Parsons

VICKA:
TOUCHED BY
A MOTHER'S LOVE

Conversations with a Medjugorje visionary

FAITH PUBLICATIONS
(IRELAND)

First published in 2002 by Faith Publications (Ireland)
Ars Sacra, Medjugorje, Bosnia-Herzegovina

First print 2002

The author recognises and accepts that the ultimate
and final authority regarding the validity of claimed
apparitions rests with the Catholic Church and the
Holy See of Rome, and willingly awaits and submits
to the final results of the ongoing investigations
into the events in Medjugorje.

The author asserts the moral right to be identified
as the author of this work.

A CIP catalogue record for this book is available
from the British Library

ISBN 0-9532777-2-0

Cover design by Alanna Corballis
Edited and typeset by Carole Devaney

CONTENTS

Introduction

It's almost seventeen years since I first set foot on the red soil of Medjugorje. Little did I know then what changes were in store for my life. In the years that followed, I have experienced tremendous blessings and much joy and peace. I have also discovered that when you decide to walk with Jesus and Mary, you open your life to great challenges and a deep scrutiny of your own response to the call of God.

Like all those included in the pages of this book, my own life has been deeply affected by the apparitions of the Mother of God in this isolated valley in the Herzegovina region of Bosnia-Herzegovina. As I wrote the final chapters, it was suggested that in the introduction I should tell the story of how my own life was changed by the happenings in this place. That story had already gained a great deal of publicity in the national press and on TV and radio in Ireland, England and the United States. I hesitated to tell it again until a priest friend suggested that it was not what I wanted, but perhaps what God wanted that was most important and that not everybody would be aware of the tremendous gift of personal conversion I had been given and should continue to share.

So, with apologies to those who already know my story, here is my own account of the graces and blessings that can pour into even the most jaded heart when faced with the reality that I believe is Medjugorje.

It was 24 June 1985, and just over seventeen years from the first day I had entered the fascinating but often cynical world of journalism, when I arrived in Medjugorje. Over those years, I had worked on national newspapers and a variety of magazines, in areas from show business to news and human interest features and investigative reports.

If anybody had asked, my reply would have been that I'd been everywhere, seen it all – from the brash unreal world of music and film stars to a private audience with Pope Paul VI in the Vatican, from stories of great human courage and achievement to those of utter degradation and inhumanity. And through most of it, I had managed to remain detached and objective.

When asked to investigate what was said to be happening in this unknown rural valley in part of what was then communist Yugoslavia, little did I know that while objectivity would be maintained, my detachment would be challenged in a way I had never before experienced.

Another factor which the news editor of the national Sunday paper for which I was working had thought relevant to the reporting of the happenings was that I was not a Catholic. Brought up as a member of the minority Church of Ireland congregation, he felt that I would bring both objectivity and a good dash of reality to my assignment, a view with which I completely agreed. And besides, the story was sure to be an interesting one – the first time a national Irish newspaper would have reported fully on the so-called apparitions claimed to be taking place.

It was extremely hot when at 4pm the driver of the car in which I was travelling pulled up close to the twin-spired church of St. James in Medjugorje and arranged to collect me again later that night to take me back to the nearby village of Čitluk where I was to sleep.

My first impressions were of the enormous crowds all around the church. Later, I discovered, over 100,000 people had gathered in the valley that day to celebrate the fourth anniversary of the apparitions of the Queen of Peace.

Making myself known to the Irish nurse who was facilitating English-speaking pilgrims visiting the parish, I asked for meetings to be arranged with the 'visionaries' and with the priests ministering to them. With a slight smile, she told me that as evening services would soon begin, perhaps I could just walk around and experience something of the atmosphere in the valley. The following morning, she promised, she would help me to organise what interviews I required.

Making a firm appointment to meet with her, I then took her advice and for the next hour or so wandered about, watching, observing and taking notes of what I saw. My first impression, from the very moment I had left the car and made my way around the church grounds, was of the total peace that seemed to prevail in this then underdeveloped place, despite the immense numbers of people. None of the usual and often unpleasant side effec of large crowds were evident – pushing, shoving and humour as everybody attempts to establish thei space.

Under trees, I saw groups of people talking or with one of the several brown-robed Frar Others sat or knelt, alone or in small g reading or talking quietly in many dif Four years after the first reports of thesf people from almost every country ir have gathered here, drawn by seemed utterly unbelievable an

Shortly before 6pm, I ma

against the right outer wall of the parish church of St. James, which stood in the middle of this valley, the focal point for the tiny hamlets dotted around and about the area. The end of June sunshine was strong and bright, and I closed my eyes as I leaned back against the heat of the stone wall. The evening services had begun, the church was packed to capacity and the crowd overflowed to the sides and front of the church, stretching way back under the trees.

Loud-speakers relayed everything, in the Croatian language, to the crowds outside and it wasn't until the following day that I discovered that the rosary was being said. Nor did I realise at the time that what I experienced just a short time later coincided with the time of the daily apparition. All I knew was that the sun was shining, the atmosphere was peaceful, my driver wouldn't return for a few hours – and I may even get the beginnings of a suntan as I turned my face, eyes closed, towards the sun that shone down so strongly from above the line of trees opposite the church wall.

Lost in the warmth and my own thoughts of who I might interview tomorrow as I began my investigations into these rather bizarre claims of apparitions, my attention was suddenly taken by the sound of children's voices, loudly and urgently calling to their parents. Looking around to see what had apparently frightened them, I realised that they were pointing up into the sky in front of me.

Lifting my hand to shade my eyes from the bright light of the sun, I followed the direction of their pointing fingers and for one short, sharp moment doubted the reality of my own sight. Closing my eyes momentarily, I looked and saw exactly the same thing. There, in the sky

above me, the sun was spinning like a giant top.

As I watched, colours appeared to come streaming from behind it – red, green, yellow, blue – to circle it independently, while all the time the sun continued to spin. Then the centre of the sun turned to red and then to black before returning to its usual brightness. Above it, slightly to the right, I suddenly saw what appeared to be white cloudlike letters begin to form. As I watched, the word 'Peace' appeared in the sky above the dancing sun – in English, but in what I would have described as Celtic script, just like that in the Book of Kells. Remaining for what seemed like twenty or thirty seconds – although to be honest I was not counting time as I witnessed this extraordinary and unbelievable phenomenon – the word disappeared and the sun continued to spin and dance.

Now and then, I tore my gaze away from it to look around at the reactions of others. Only seconds after the amazing spectacle began, I had realised that I had no need to shade my eyes, but could look at the sun clearly, something that seemed physically impossible under other circumstances. Those around me were also watching, wide-eyed and apparently experiencing the same extraordinary scene. Others walking by stared at those looking up into the sky, looked up in the same direction themselves and, while some stopped and stared in apparent amazement or even disbelief, others looked back at us, shook their heads and walked on, quite obviously not seeing anything at all unusual.

At one stage, as I continued to stare up towards the sky in an experience that lasted some thirty-five minutes, the spinning sun with its surrounding swirling colours seemed to break away from the heavens to come rushing towards us. All round me, I heard cries of fear mingled with terror-filled prayers, as the sun's brightness came closer and closer until all I could see was a total golden light. Strangely, I realised, I felt no fear before the descent of light stopped and then withdrew back into the sky, where the sun continued to spin.

It was just after this that the one part of this phenomenon that would have a real and lasting effect on my life occurred. As I continued to stare at the sun, I saw what seemed like a fountain of light gush up from it. Just as with a fountain of water, where it reached its highest point this fountain of light separated and there appeared, to my utter astonishment, a bright, shining figure with arms outstretched. So bright and shining that I could never describe the whiteness of the garment, but a figure that I immediately recognised, despite my own lack of religious interest for many years, as the Risen Christ.

So clear was this shining figure that I could even see the sleeves that hung from the wrists to flow down to meet the hem of the garment where it touched the feet. But I could not see the face. Try as I might, I could not make out the features on the face, although I knew it was there, framed by hair that fell to the shoulders.

All around me, people were pulling at my arms and asking, 'Do you see the Host coming up out of the sun?' Knowing nothing of the Host, I kept replying 'No. But do you see the figure coming out of the sun?'

Ten times this figure disappeared, to return again almost immediately, always preceded by the fountain of light. At one point I recall holding my hand in front of my face – and continuing to see the figure as if my hand was not there.

And then the realisation, as I stood in this place and continued to look up into the sky, that tears were pouring down my face and the only thought in my mind was that I was in the presence of God.

Afterwards, when the sun resumed its natural and still position in the sky, I spoke to almost three dozen people who had been standing close by me, asking what their experience had been, but not mentioning my own. Each one had undergone much the same experience, seeing the sun spin, the colours come around it, and most had witnessed its inexplicable rush towards earth. Some claimed to have seen the figure of a woman holding a child in the centre of its brightness, others to have seen a cross. None had seen the word 'Peace'.

But the most surprising thing, for me, was that no one made any mention of seeing the shining figure I had repeatedly witnessed.

It was only after my return home that somebody close to me said quietly, and with utter conviction, 'But do you not realise what happened? Those others saw the Host come up out of the sun and recognised Jesus in it. You saw the Body because you had no concept of the Host'.

It was a realisation that in time was to completely change my life.

In the days that followed this extraordinary experience, for which I could find no logical explanation and finally was forced to conclude could therefore only be supernatural, I put it to the back of my mind and set about interviewing visionaries, priests and others. What I found was honesty, sincerity and a deep spirituality, and the realisation that the reported apparitions of this Queen of Peace had undoubtedly changed the lives of not only all those who lived in this valley, but the millions who were now visiting it.

What I had expected to find, as I made plans to travel here, was Marian propaganda. What I discovered, instead, was the Gospel message. 'Turn back to my Son', they reported the Virgin as saying. 'Convert. Confess. Pray. Fast. Change your lives'. It was a Mother's call that appeared to find a heartfelt response in almost every person who visited this valley.

It was a week after returning home when I finally sat down to write the story of what I found in Medjugorje, a story that was very different to the one I had visualised as I travelled there. What would I write, I had agonised – a report on the alleged apparitions with quotes from the so-called visionaries? Or the very personal story of what I had found and experienced in this valley?

In the end, my years of training and experience decided the issue. Right through my career, I had reported factually as I found each situation or each subject. I could do no different here, although one small part of my mind continued to warn me that many might find it difficult or impossible to accept the truth of my report, thus destroying the credibility of my career to date.

In the end, truth won out and the report that I filed was a full account of not only the happenings said to be taking place in Medjugorje, but of my own extraordinary and very personal experience just a couple of hours after arriving there.

After the resultant publicity, this should have been the end of the story, but in fact it was only the beginning. Left with the realisation that I had been brought face to face with the reality of God's existence, I was left also with a choice. How would I respond to this reality?

All of my life, if asked, I would have called myself a Christian. Now, I began to realise, to be a Christian meant to have and to keep Christ in the centre of one's life. Left with so many questions in my mind, I found myself being drawn inexorably towards the Roman Catholic faith.

Joining a prayer group in the Dublin Catholic parish in which I lived, I met a wonderful Spirit-filled priest called Fr. Aidan Carroll, whose deep faith and utter honesty and integrity had a powerful influence on my own spiritual life. Three and a half years later, on 8 December 1988, the Feast of the Immaculate Conception, I was received into the Roman Catholic Church, the total belief and faith I had come to have in the Real Presence of Jesus in the Eucharist being the foundation on which I built my new life.

Now I too recognised Him in the Host, just as those around me did on that June evening in a much-blessed place called Medjugorje.

Heather Parsons
March 2002

Acknowledgements

With heartfelt thanks to all those who helped, advised, encouraged me and by so doing made it possible for me to write this book.

To Peter and to my children and their children – without your love, support and prayers my life would be incomplete.

To the many wonderful and Spirit-filled priests I have met over my seventeen years' involvement with the happenings of Medjugorje, both there and at home, especially Fr. Aidan Carroll, Fr. Liam Lawton, Fr. Paddy Devine, Fr. Michael O'Carroll, Fr. Paddy Byrne, Fr. Peter Rookey, Fr. Svetozar Kralijec and the late Fr. Slavko Barbarić.

To Major General Liam Prendergast, who has made such a vital contribution to the orderly and factual dissemination of information about the happenings of Medjgorje in Ireland.

To all those tireless group leaders, including Tony Carroll, who have worked to spread the message of the Gospa and to take others to experience her presence in Medjugorje.

To Tom Field and all those in Marian Pilgrimages, Dublin, who have continued to make it possible, even through the worst of the war years in Bosnia-Herzegovina, for pilgrims to visit and experience Medjugorje in a deeply prayerful way.

To Joanna, who prays constantly for me.

To Ante Mužić, who first asked Vicka if she would work with me on this book.

To Marija Jerković and Paula Wade Mužić, B.A. Theol., who spent so many hours patiently interpreting.

To Carole Devaney and Alanna Corballis for their editing and design skills.

To all of those who trusted me with the stories of their lives as told within the pages of this book.

And, most especially, to Vicka Ivanković who shared so willingly with me her personal experience of the words and the love and the constant call of the Mother of God through her daily apparitions in Medjugorje.

For my family and friends,
whose love and prayers mean more
than I could ever say.

But especially for the Queen of Peace,
who took me by the hand and led me
to her Son in the Eucharist.

Chapter 1

The Gospa's call

A sharp frost covers the valley, glistening on rooftops and bushes and ice-covered puddles.

From the balcony of Vicka's family home, Bijakovići looks peaceful and still sleepy. Little stirs the calm, apart from a few scratching hens and the inevitable crowing of a disgruntled cockerel.

From the house opposite comes an old woman dressed in traditional black, pail in hand. Moving slowly to the hen-house near by, she coaxes out the reluctant inhabitants with handfuls of meal. The hens fed, she picks up a broom and takes it inside. In the cold early-morning air, clouds of dust and chaff and feathers float out to disappear slowly, wafting their way lazily down the hillside.

Across the valley, the first rays of pale winter sunshine begin to pick out the track leading up Križevac. High on its peak, the huge stone cross is clearly visible, standing guard over the villages dotted around its feet, just as it has for the last sixty-eight years.

Leaning against the balcony railing, it's easy to imagine this tiny village just as it was over twenty years ago, before some of the most momentous events ever to be recorded were even imagined.

And who, then, could have imagined what was to come! Who could have foretold how the names of the valley of Medjugorje and this tiny hamlet of Bijakovići, that great rocky mountain – renamed when the cross was erected

– and the hill of Podbrdo, right behind this house, would one day be known right across the Catholic world and beyond? How the experiences of six young people and their daily contact with a beautiful Mother would touch the hearts of millions and lead them to the Son of God?

In the house behind me, Vicka Ivanković is praying with a young Italian girl and her family. The child is seriously ill – just one of the many who come here to plead that their suffering might be presented to the Mother of God, whose Son can surely deny her nothing.

As they leave, tears of hope pouring down their faces, I look down into the yard and realise that while I stood here gazing across the valley, dozens of people had made their way silently through the gate and were staring up at the balcony, hoping to meet with the woman who, for over twenty years, has had a unique and love-filled relationship with the same Mary who stood at the foot of her Son's cross.

Seconds later, Vicka leaves the house and goes down to meet the pilgrims. As she stands on the lower steps and begins to lead the fast-growing crowd in prayer, I leave the coldness of the balcony and seek shelter in the house.

Inside, all is still. In the back room where, for much of the last twenty years, Vicka has had her daily meetings with the Gospa, as she is called in the local Croatian language, a sense of peace and stillness is not just imagined.

Silently, I look about me. With its brown and beige carpet, plain couch and two chairs covered with thick white fringed cloths, I could be standing in any of the older houses in this tiny village. The inevitable coffee table sits in

2

the centre of the room and a small bookcase against the back wall is crammed with a mixture of books, pictures, religious objects and candles.

But it's to the opposite wall that my eyes are drawn – to the old carved sideboard with its white embroidered cloth on top, completely covered with a mass of flowers, petitions and bags of religious objects. To either side of these stands a statue. To the right, Jesus of the Sacred Heart. To the left, a slightly smaller statue of the Gospa, in white with a blue sash and a crown on her head. From her folded hands hang rosaries and scapulars, and in front of her a crib with the baby Jesus lying in the straw. Dominating the wall behind is a large crucifix, casting its shadow across the crib.

My eyes focus on the crucifix.

It is here, almost every evening, that the Mother of God comes. For over twenty years . . . for love of the whole world . . . for love of me.

The enormity of it all strikes me anew as tears, unbidden, fill my eyes. And in one of those strange, sudden moments of joy, a wonderful feeling of peace overwhelms me.

From outside, I hear Vicka's voice.

"You say – I cannot pray today. I am too tired. But just as our bodies cannot live without water, our souls cannot live without prayer.

"I cannot fast? Our Lady says that if we fast out of love for her and her son, Jesus, it will be possible.

"To those who do not feel Jesus and Mary close, Our Lady says – 'We are always close to you. But you have to open your hearts to us'.

"We ask, what can we give up? Most of all, we can give up sin.

"Conversion. Confession. The Eucharist. These are the foundations for our lives. And this is a time of great grace.

"Are we ready to receive that grace?"

It is almost an hour later before the last pilgrim has left the small yard and the gate is closed over.

Despite the watery sunshine, there is little heat in the January morning air. But not even the long time spent standing on the cold stone steps has taken the warmth from Vicka's smile. A smile that lights up not only her eyes, but her whole face and finds its roots in a deep inner peace and joy.

It's this inner tranquillity that allows her, despite years of ill health, to give totally of herself to all who come here. To stand, endlessly, with patience and love, and talk and pray with people from a dozen different countries. To never refuse to meet with them each morning, whether in teeming rain or scorching sun. And to leave each one feeling that they have experienced something special and challenging in their own lives.

This morning, I had noticed she prayed not only with the pilgrims as a group, but also individually. Almost every person standing in the yard – and the dozens who stood outside the wall, unable to get in until others left – had come towards her for personal contact. Other days, she had prayed only over the group, although for an extended length of time.

Why does this vary?

As with many questions, her initial response is a smile and a brief shrug of her shoulders. In this, and all else in her life, she is led greatly by the Spirit.

"Sometimes, people ask for personal contact," she says simply.

"They say, 'Vicka, you are so close to Our Lady – at least touch my head', and then I pray over them.

"But first of all, it is very important to give the words of Our Lady, of her messages, so that their hearts are opened. And then I try to bring that prayer closer to them, into their own lives so that they can feel it in their lives."

Again, this morning, she had mentioned something to the pilgrims that I had heard her saying some months before to another group.

"It concerned a special intention of Our Lady's," I remind Vicka. "You asked us to pray especially for one specific intention which, you said, would soon be fulfilled."

She nods her head, replying immediately.

"That is true, and you heard me recommend the same thing to the group this morning.

"Recently, Our Lady said this to me, that she wanted each one of us to pray for her intentions, one of which, she said, would soon become true. But no, she did not say which intention she was talking of.

"She only asked that we especially pray for its fulfilment because, as she has told us over the years, it is only with our prayer that her intentions for the world can be fulfilled.

"This special one, I believe, she will explain a little later on and then, when it comes true, we will see.

"For me, it is enough for now that she has asked us to pray for peace and for her special intentions, and that we do as she has asked."

The Gospa's call to prayer is central to the huge spiritual happenings in this isolated valley in a rural area of Bosnia-Herzegovina.

In those very first days following the unannounced appearance on the hill of Podbrdo of a 'beautiful woman' on 24 June 1981, the feast day of St. John the Baptist, prayer was at the centre of everything.

Unsure as how to behave towards the Virgin – who the young visionaries recognised instantly within their hearts and who on the third day, when they asked, identified herself with the words 'I am the Blessed Virgin Mary' – they were drawn irresistibly towards the long-used prayers of their families.

They prayed Our Fathers, Hail Marys and Glory Bes, they said, as they awaited the Gospa's return each evening because these were the prayers that came most naturally to them.

They asked the advice of the women of their village, and they, too, recommended the saying of the seven Our Fathers, Hail Marys and Glory Bes.

Soon after, they asked the Gospa herself, who told them to persist with the seven recitals of these prayers for the sick and for peace in the world, and to add to these the Creed.

And as the Gospa continued to talk and pray with the six young people on a daily basis over the following weeks, months and years, her constant call continued to be for prayer. Prayer from the heart. Prayer for conversion. Prayer for peace 'in this peaceless world'.

Her messages came at first on a daily basis to the visionaries, who made them known to the parish, from where they spread to the whole world. Then, later on, she gave them on a weekly basis (from 1 March 1984) and subsequently each month (from 25 January 1987 to the present day). Through these messages, the Gospa called mankind to personal conversion – through prayer, confession, fasting and the Eucharist.

It's a call that has remained constant over almost twenty-one years.

But has it been heard?

"Dear Children," she said over three years later, on 8 November 1984.

"You are not conscious of the messages which God is sending you through me. He is giving you great graces and you do not comprehend them. Pray to the Holy Spirit for enlightenment. If you only knew how great are the graces God is granting you, you would be praying without ceasing. Thank you for having responded to my call."

On 25 February 2002, the call to prayer and conversion was as heartfelt:

"Dear Children. In this time of grace, I call you to become friends of Jesus. Pray for peace in your hearts and work for your personal conversion. Little children, only in this way will you be able to become witnesses of peace and of the love of Jesus in the world. Open yourselves to prayer, so that prayer becomes a need for you. Be converted, little children, and work so that as many souls as possible may come to know Jesus and His love. I am close to you and I bless you all. Thank you for having responded to my call."

But have we responded, I now ask?

Is Our Lady disappointed with our response to her call over all these years?

Vicka's face grows serious.

"She is sad," she says slowly.

"She says, 'I have so many messages to give you, but I cannot give them to you because the messages I have already given are not received'.

"She says, 'I am looking forward to every pilgrim who comes here, but I am most of all happy when you go back to your homes and give the messages with joy to others'.

"She says that many times we accept the messages, all of a sudden, and then we get tired later and nothing happens. And Our Lady says, 'I would be most happy if you received the messages with your heart and every day decide to live them going step by step forward'."

In the stillness of the room, I realise the inadequacy of my own response. Days and weeks of joy and commitment, before the fire fades and the pressures of daily life take centre place once again.

I am reminded, too, of something Archbishop Murillo Krieger from Brazil said when, during a three-day visit to Medjugorje in February 1988, he preached in the parish church of St. James at evening Mass.

He saw Medjugorje as a gift, but also a responsibility, he told those listening.

A gift – and a grace.

"Our Lady gives to everyone who comes here the possibility to find the same love and tenderness that she revealed in Cana of Galilee," he said.

"Our Lady comes close to us and asks of us to 'Do all that He tells you'. And the servants in Cana of Galilee did everything asked of them and they filled up the jars with water.

"Thus, it was possible for Jesus to work His first miracle in Cana.

"If our hearts had been open and ready to walk in the way of Christ, everything that the Lord wanted to do through Medjugorje would have already been done.

"Is it really that hard to give our hearts to Jesus Christ?"

So many of us come to Medjugorje searching for God, I observe to Vicka. But does Our Lady say what is the best way to find Him?

"Of course!" The smile has returned, its confidence and joy lighting up the shadowy room.

"She says that the best way to find Him is to open our hearts and to search for Him with our hearts, if we truly want to meet God with the heart.

"But that decision has to be ours, she says, because God gave us free will. He gave us total freedom and through that freedom we can do whatever we want.

"So the decision to find Him is ours alone. But when we truly search for Him with our hearts, He is always there, waiting."

Vicka Ivanković's response to the call of Jesus and His mother remains as deeply committed and heartfelt today as it did on that very first momentous day when she saw the figure of a woman on the hillside behind her home.

It was some time after five o'clock in the afternoon, she recalls. Despite the fact that it was a feast day, Vicka had to take the bus to the town of Mostar some 30 kilometres away, to take mathematics grinds for an upcoming exam. On her way home, the bus was uncomfortably hot and crowded, and she was relieved when she eventually arrived back in Bijakovići around mid-day.

Soon after reaching her house, two close friends, Ivanka Ivanković and Mirjana Dragicević, called by to arrange to meet up later for a walk when the heat of the day had passed. After this Vicka made herself a light meal, then lay down on her bed, where she fell soundly asleep.

It was cooler when her older sister, Zdenka, woke her.

Dressing quickly, Vicka went in search of Mirjana and Ivanka, going first to Jakov Čolo's house where his mother, Mirjana's aunt, said they had already headed off up the road for a walk.

Following the same path, Vicka suddenly saw the two girls, and little Milka Pavlović, staring at something which seemed to have greatly frightened them. They waved urgently at her to come up the hill and Vicka, seeing their fear, began to hurry towards them. As she approached, the three began to shout, "Vicka – the Virgin – look!"

Vicka turned and ran back down the road at great speed, only stopping to take off her slippers so that she could run faster.

Reaching the village, she struggled to catch her breath, then began to cry. What were the others up to? Why were they talking about a Virgin?

Just then, two boys came by – Ivan Dragicević, carrying a bag full of apples, and another Ivan. Rejecting the offer of an apple, Vicka told them that something strange was going on – that the other girls were claiming to have seen the Virgin. She asked Ivan Dragicević would he go back with her to investigate.

When they arrived back, the three other girls began to point up behind them on the hillside. Vicka and Ivan looked up and suddenly they, too, saw the figure. Ivan immediately took to his heels, dropping the apples as he ran. This time, however, Vicka stayed.

What she saw, she said afterwards, was the shining figure of a 'beautiful maiden' holding a child in her arms. Continually covering and then uncovering the child, as if she wished them to see him, she beckoned the five to approach her.

None of them dared. They were not even sure of exactly

how long they stood there, staring at the beautiful woman – perhaps only minutes – before running away, back down the hilly road.

Vicka recalled sitting down on the couch in her home, where she 'cried and cried'.

That evening, the children related all they had seen to their families. Before long, the news had spread up and down the little village of Bijakovići and beyond. Some scoffed at the story. Others believed. Some even thought it was some kind of unidentified flying object.

Every conceivable theory was put forward before the village finally settled into an uneasy sleep, not too many hours before dawn broke and the usual chores of caring for the animals and harvesting the wine and tobacco crops would again begin.

All night, Vicka said, she tossed and turned, but when she slept she dreamt of the shining figure of the beautiful lady.

Something in their hearts drew the children up the hillside again the following day.

Vicka, Ivanka and Mirjana discussed what had happened and agreed to go back to the same place on the hill at about the same time of day. If it really were the Virgin, they reasoned, perhaps she would come again.

Shortly after five o'clock, they began to make their way back up the gravel road leading around the hillside. Vicka, Ivanka and Mirjana led the way, with Marija Pavlović and little Jakov Čolo following some way behind. Marija's younger sister, Milka, was not allowed to go as she had to do chores for her mother. On their way, they were joined by Ivan Dragicević, with a number of others from the village following at a distance.

As they reached the same place on the road, they

looked up the hillside to where, the previous day, they had seen the shining figure. Suddenly, a bright light shone and the Lady appeared, this time without the child.

Again, as on the previous day, Ivanka was the first to see her. As promised, Vicka immediately called Marija and Jakov. When the Lady waved her hand to beckon them forward, Vicka recalls, they all immediately ran towards her – Marija and Jakov too, although they did not see the figure immediately, and Ivan, who instinctively followed the others.

Even today, they are not totally sure of how they managed to get up the overgrown hillside. Feeling as if something was propelling them forward, they ran directly through thorny bushes and over the stony ground until they reached the top of the hill where the figure waited. Falling on their knees, the six children, then aged between ten and seventeen, began to pray. Vicka recalled seeing little Jakov fall right into a thorny thicket, but there wasn't a mark on him when he pulled himself out.

The Lady was 'beautiful, smiling, happy', Vicka later said, wearing a long grey dress, which covered her feet, and a white veil on her head. Her hair was black and curled a little where it hung down beneath the veil. Her eyes were blue, her face 'longish' and her lips and cheeks were rosy in colour. Above her head was a crown of twelve stars. When she appeared she was preceded by a bright light.

She was so beautiful, Vicka said, but not in a way that could be described with words. A beauty that went beyond that of the world.

She smiled and prayed with the children. Ivanka asked about her mother, who had died some weeks before. The Lady told her that her mother was well, that she was with her, and that Ivanka had no need to worry.

Before she left, the children asked whether she would come to them again. She nodded that she would, finally leaving them with the farewell, 'Goodbye, my angels'.

It was the second evening of a relationship that would continue to this day.

At the time of writing, March 2002, Vicka Ivanković still continues to see the Blessed Virgin Mary without fail every evening. Marija Pavlović and Ivan Dragicević also continue to have daily apparitions, while Ivanka, Mirjana and Jakov, who have already received their ten special messages, or 'secrets', from the Queen of Peace (as she later called herself) now only see her on certain special occasions as decided by the Gospa herself. Vicka, Marija and Ivan have received nine such messages.

Today, wherever she is – whether at home in Medjugorje or elsewhere, Vicka confirms – the Gospa appears to her at 5.40pm (6.40pm summer time).

"Only when I am travelling, perhaps by airplane, is it different. Then it is always before I travel. But otherwise, it is never at any other time of the day."

Does she have advance warning of the apparition?

"Yes, always, in my heart." Her eyes are full of joy and happiness as she relives those moments.

"It is such a special feeling that you cannot describe it with words. There are just no words to describe it. But I always prepare myself, through prayer, for the coming of Our Lady. And when she comes, she does not come suddenly, physically – but instead, I slowly begin to feel her coming, in my heart, before she finally arrives."

Even after almost twenty-one years, describing her

feelings during these apparitions does not come easily.

"It is such a very special feeling – as if you are not on earth. As if you are floating on air. And afterwards, you have to come back to the reality, but that joy stays, the joy of the meeting with her.

"And if you choose to accept the messages Our Lady gives, then you just keep on living that joy."

The length of time the Gospa stays still varies, as it has over those years.

"Sometimes she remains only five minutes, sometimes ten, fifteen or twenty. I never know how long she will remain – that is her decision."

During the apparition, Vicka confirms, the Virgin appears just as any human would – not as if in a picture or in any hazy way, but fully alive. Over the years, she has prayed with Vicka, laughed with her, spoken at length and held her in her arms.

In the early days, it was reported that the Gospa often held and hugged and kissed the young visionaries.

"Yes, that is still true today," Vicka smiles.

"Especially for birthdays. Our Lady has a very special feeling for birthdays, and always on both her birthday and our own we congratulate each other in this way."

What it must be like to be held in the arms of the Mother of God seems unimaginable to me.

"It is indescribable," Vicka agrees.

"When she holds you or when she just gives you a hug – it is just impossible to describe the feeling. We talk about these things, but still it is not possible to describe the feeling inside. I have tried, so many times, to describe that feeling of joy, the unbelievable happiness, but no words are sufficient.

"And if you ask me what is the most beautiful thing

about her, I can only answer – everything, because it is impossible to say anything else.

"Once, when we asked her why she was so beautiful, she smiled and said 'Because I love! You should start to love, and then you will become beautiful'.

"She is such a beautiful Mother, so full of love – for all of us, not especially for us visionaries, but for all people.

"So often she has told us that she is the Mother of all, even of those who do not accept her. That her only wish is to lead all people to her Son."

Chapter 2

A Mother's touch

On 25 April 1998, the Gospa gave the following message:

"Dear Children. Today I call you, through prayer, to open yourselves to God as a flower opens itself to the rays of the morning sun. Little children, do not be afraid. I am with you and I intercede before God for each of you, so that your heart receives the gift of conversion. Only in this way, little children, will you comprehend the importance of grace in these times, and God will become nearer to you. Thank you for having responded to my call."

Herbert Fuchs stood at the foot of the mountain and looked up. High above him he saw the shape of the great stone cross, its greyness reflecting the desolation he felt inside himself.

What he was doing here he still did not know. Three days after arriving, he was no happier than when he had first stepped off the bus.

He felt tense, uptight, his stomach seemingly tied in a knot. The curiosity that had led him here now seemed impossible to understand. Much of it was to do with missing his wife, he reasoned. She had been supposed to travel with him, but a throat infection at the last moment had put pay to that. So he had travelled alone. And was missing her terribly.

When he had reached the bus that would travel from

Austria across and down into Bosnia-Herzegovina, he found himself praying that his name wouldn't be on the list, that he could return home. But no – there it was and he couldn't think of anything else to do but get on the bus.

Twenty-four hours later, without having slept a wink, he stepped onto the red soil outside the house in Medjugorje in which he would stay. To his left, the twin spires of the church of St. James looked exactly like the pictures he had been shown.

He'd been interested then, his curiosity hugely aroused by the friend who had told him of his visit and his strange experience right here in this village. A military pilot – and quite a character who loved the good life and women just a little too much – this friend had travelled to Medjugorje at the plea of his wife. While there, he told Herbert, he had climbed a large mountain named Križevac. And on the mountain, he had undergone a strange experience during which he had been clearly shown the evil of his life.

On his return from Medjugorje, he was totally changed. When Herbert heard the details of this experience, he immediately booked the tickets to see this place for himself.

Now he wondered just what had got into him.

Rash decisions were not part of his life. Holding a senior position within the Austrian State Justice Department, his approach to both work and life was serious and well thought out. Impulse and irrationality were not part of his nature. Or if they were, he had learned to overcome them during a youth that had been both painful and lonely.

Now, standing at the foot of the same mountain of Križevac in 1998, that pain and loneliness swept back into his mind, overpowering every other emotion.

His mother – his heart was full of the pain she had caused him.

He had been only five years old when she had given him away. He remembered her, but not his father. He'd never seen his father. But the day his mother gave him away – because she was alone and could no longer cope with life – felt as raw in his mind now as it had all those years ago.

At the time, there had been a State grant for families who would foster children. The frightened child had been placed with one of these. What he found there was shelter, but no love or justice. Even at this age, he felt the pain of being treated differently by his foster mother to her natural children.

His life there left him emotionally scarred and with little respect for Christianity. His foster-mother attended Mass regularly, but even as a child Herbert realised that the lack of love she displayed for him was completely at variance with the supposed core of her religion.

Every moment since then, he had felt this aching void inside him – the lack of a mother's loving touch in his life. He had learned to live without it, he had thought, and the love of his wife had brought great happiness. But still, deep inside him remained that emptiness, the cry of a small child for its mother.

And now, here it was again, back to haunt him as he looked up towards the top of the mountain. Right inside his inner being, Herbert Fuchs felt a deep sadness. He began to climb the mountain and as he did so, he now recalls, he felt the tension relax. Half-way up, he stopped to look down into the valley and realised that the sick feeling in his stomach had subsided.

He prefers not to go into details about the experience he had when he finally reached the top of the mountain. All he will say is that it was a sign, in the sky, after which everything else took on an enormous significance. And a voice, deep inside him, telling him that he would return to the mountain.

Later, back near the church, Herbert found himself drawn into one of the souvenir shops where he suddenly saw, high on a shelf, a statue of the Gospa. For some strange reason, he says, he knew he had to have the statue.

"When I told the assistant that I wanted to buy this statue, she went back into the store room and brought out one that was already packed in a box," he recollects now with a smile.

"She was rather taken aback when I said no, that I wanted this particular statue on the shelf. As soon as I bought it, I put it into my rucksack and went into the church. The statue was so big that it couldn't fit into the bag completely, and the head was sticking out.

"Afterwards, instead of returning to the house, I told one of the group members that I was going back up Križevac."

On his way towards the mountain, one of the straps on the rucksack broke under the weight of the statue. Herbert hesitated, then decided that he wasn't going to let this stop him. Continuing on, he reached the foot of the mountain.

It was Good Friday.

Even now, he becomes emotional when he looks back on that heartfelt climb.

"The wind was blowing and it was raining and it was cold. At times, I was hardly able to move with the cold. The climb was such a struggle. And at one stage, I fell."

Before this, he says, he had never really prayed – not from the heart. Now he found himself kneeling in front of each station, crying and praying with all his heart.

"And as I prayed and cried, it felt as if all the weight

I had been carrying in my heart up to this was falling away, and my heart was getting lighter and lighter."

It was an experience that Bishop John Baptist Odama of Uganda would have identified with. Visiting Medjugorje in Spring 1996, only a couple of months after being ordained Bishop, he spoke of his own personal reaction to the events, including the day he climbed Križevac.

It had started to rain and afterwards to hail, as he and others began to climb.

"At one point I thought it was better to return because it seemed pointless to go on. However, something urged me onwards.

"I thought that I wouldn't be able to get to the top. I felt a heaviness, because I hadn't gone anywhere on foot for so long. We didn't want to turn back, but to go on was so hard. At one moment, I prayed for strength so that I wouldn't give up.

"I have to admit that when, completely wet, we arrived beneath the cross on Križevac, all at once every heaviness and tiredness left me. I felt as light as a bird."

The experience, he said, was very important to him.

"This is how it is in life too. Often we feel that we can't go on, that it's too difficult, but when we succumb to the will of God, everything goes well."

About half-way up the mountain, Herbert lifted his head and looked at the cross marking the station.

"It was broken in places and in bad condition, as if it wasn't being looked after, and this anger welled up inside me. I looked at this cross of Christ and I said to myself, it should not be like that. Why doesn't somebody do something about that? And it was as if a voice suddenly spoke back to me and said, 'Well, will you do something?' And I found myself answering – 'I will!'"

His heart was strangely lighter when he reached the top of the mountain. He took the statue out of the rucksack and placed it on the ledge beneath the cross. With difficulty he lit two candles, but the wind was howling and it was raining and so cold that he finally had to put the statue back into the rucksack and walk down the mountain.

"When I got to the bottom, it was the strangest most puzzling experience because I suddenly realised that the weather was once again warmer and quite nice. I remember thinking, 'I want to go back up again'. And as I looked at the statue sticking up out of the rucksack, it was as if it was glowing. And everything in my heart and my mind suddenly seemed much clearer."

Again, he set off up the mountain and again, as he climbed, the weather seemed unaccountably to close in on him. Reaching the top, he tried to find shelter over to one side of the huge stone cross, but here, too, the wind was howling and the rain lashing against him. Looking at the statue, he recalls saying to it, somewhat ruefully, 'Could you not see that this is not the place for us?' before heading back down the mountain.

But that was not the end of his climb to faith, he now recalls quietly.

Once again, the weather had improved immensely by the time he reached the bottom of the mountain. And inside him was a compelling urge to take the statue back up again.

Responding instinctively to this, Herbert found himself once again climbing the mountain. About half-way up, the weather again turned treacherous. Climbing with difficulty in the wind and rain, and wondering just what madness had made him think he should come up again, he heard the sound of something knocking on metal. Three times.

Curious, he lifted his head to see a rosary hanging from a cross beside the station, knocking against it in the howling wind. For some reason, he says, he found himself reaching out to lift the rosary and place it around his neck. As he did this, he recalls, there were two huge flashes of lightening in the sky and again he felt as if every worry was being lifted from him.

Climbing on, he became aware once more of the deterioration of the crosses along the way and how the wind and rain and sun over the years had all but obliterated the pictures of Christ's journey to Calvary.

Again he thought how terrible their condition was and how they should be renewed or replaced.

And again, he says now quietly and convincingly, he heard a voice inside him saying 'Are you going to do it?'

It was dark by the time he left the top of the mountain for the valley below. Pitch dark, he recalls, but despite the lack of light and the difficult stony path he barely stumbled.

On the way down, he met a young man who was relieved to have company, explaining that once before he had got dreadfully lost in the dark on Križevac. And it struck Herbert as strange that he himself seemed to find his way so effortlessly.

When they reached the bottom of the mountain, he turned to the young man and suggested that they climb back up once again – 'for the Mother'.

"He looked at me and asked was I out of my mind, and I realised that despite how crazy it seemed to him, I was strangely happy about going back up there again. So I did!"

The climb this time was different, he says. The wind

still howled and the rain lashed against his body, but he felt full of life and love and happiness, and all sorts of emotions that he had never really experienced before in the deep well of pain and sadness that had always seemed to be at the core of his life.

And all along the way, he looked at the crosses and realised that he must do something about them.

Despite the weather, the time spent on top of the mountain, he says, was full of joy and healing. He felt as if a burden that he had carried all his life had been lifted by loving hands.

It was on the way back down this time, however, that he suddenly experienced a sense of something wrong.

"I had this strange and unpleasant feeling as if somebody was following me. I almost didn't want to look around, but when I finally did I saw what looked like a dark shadow behind me. Nobody spoke, but every time I looked back, this dark shadow was there. And at one stage it crossed my mind that if it wasn't another human, then it could only be the evil one.

"But almost immediately the thought came into my mind – 'Why should I be afraid of any demon? I've got my Mother here with me'.

"And that's when it struck me.

"I really did have a Mother, one who loved me like I'd never been loved before. One who would never leave me.

"And it was from that moment that I got to know my real Mother, the one who came and filled that empty place in my heart."

Herbert Fuchs' experience is one that many others have had in this isolated valley, touched by a Mother's love.

In August 1995, a retired Italian Archbishop and exorcist visited Medjugorje. Before he left, he spoke movingly about his time there.

He had come to Medjugorje not as a theologian, nor critic, nor Bishop, he said. Instead, he had come as a pilgrim, for the salvation of his soul.

"I come as a believer who has accepted Mary as my Mother. She is really a Mother. I learned this when I lost my own mother. I was only seventeen. When I spoke to a priest he told me, 'Now you have another Mother. Go to the Marian altar and tell her', and since then she is my Mother."

Was it a coincidence that Herbert Fuchs received such a wealth of motherly love into his life on Good Friday, the day the crucified Christ gave His own Mother to be the mother of all?

A gentle smile lights Herbert's eyes, but he does not feel the need to speculate. Suffice to say that the experience of motherly love still fills his heart.

His wife noticed it as soon as he returned home. Without his saying a word, she could see a huge change in him. So she came with him in August of that year to assist him in a special project.

The day after climbing Križevac five times (because he went up once again, to give thanks for all the joy and healing), Herbert climbed the mountain to place fresh pictures of the Passion over those that were no longer discernible. Later, he approached Fr. Slavko Barbarić and asked permission to first paint and then replace the crosses. Fr. Slavko, he recalls, looked closely at him for a couple of minutes, then patted him on the head and made the sign of the cross on his forehead.

No words passed between them, Herbert recalls, because none were needed. And without a murmur, the normally cautious priests of the parish of Medjugorje accepted Herbert's offer.

The crosses that now mark Christ's Good Friday journey of love to the pilgrims who climb Križevac stand strong and tall. But the old crosses have found a new mission. When Herbert Fuchs removed those worn by years of sun, wind and rain, and the touch of numerous hands, he had no plans to discard them. Instead, he brought them home, where he had them embedded into new wood and erected right across Austria to make what is probably the longest Way of the Cross in the world.

On 31 December 2001, he climbed Križevac again, close to midnight, as he has done on every New Year's Eve since 1998, to pray for the passing of the old year and the coming of the new. Sitting on the top of the mountain, in the shadow of the great cross, oblivious to the frost and freezing temperatures around him, he lit a little oil lamp and prayed – for all those in the valley below and for those all over the world in need of a Mother's love.

In his heart he carried the message of that Mother, given to the world through Marija Pavlović just days before, on 25 December 2001:

"Dear Children," she had said with immense love.

"I call you today and encourage you to prayer for peace. Especially today I call you, carrying the newborn Jesus in my arms for you, to unite with Him through prayer and to become a

sign to this peaceless world. Encourage each other, little children, to prayer and love. May your faith be an encouragement to others to believe and to love more. I bless you all, and call you to be closer to my heart and to the heart of little Jesus. Thank you for having responded to my call."

Chapter 3

The gift of suffering

The new year has arrived, but all over Medjugorje Christmas lights still twinkle from windows or light up cribs.

Watched over by his Mother, the baby Jesus lies silently in the crib, close to where I sit with Vicka. A faint smile touches His lips and the little hands reach out towards us.

The Christmas message rings through my mind, given by the Gospa who came carrying the newborn Jesus in her arms – as she has every Christmas since she first appeared in Medjugorje, I ask Vicka?

"Yes, every time at Christmas she appears with the baby Jesus, and she is so happy. He is just as you would see any little baby and she holds Him so gently in her arms and covers Him with part of her veil, just like any mother would. But her happiness is so great."

It is over twenty years since the Gospa first appeared on the rocky hillside, holding the baby Jesus in her arms. The second time she brought the child to the visionaries was on the date celebrated as the nativity of Our Lady – 8 September – in that very first year of the apparitions. On each occasion, then and since, Vicka describes the Gospa as 'exceptionally happy'.

But she has also appeared with the man Jesus?

"Only once," she replies, the smile replaced with a look

of great seriousness.

"It was on Good Friday and when the Gospa came she appeared with Jesus."

He did not speak, says Vicka, deep sadness filling her normally smiling eyes.

"But just to see Him was enough. His clothes were torn and His face was so marked and full of blood. His body was wounded and on His head was the crown of thorns.

"And the Gospa said, 'I come to show you how much Jesus suffered for you – for all of you'."

The pain and shock of witnessing His agony was enormous, says Vicka.

"But Our Lady gives us special strength in these moments so that we can witness what we see to other people.

"We felt so bad. We pitied Jesus so much to see Him like that – so torn, with blood all over Him – but Our Lady was there to give us strength to bear it, so that we could tell this terrible thing to others.

"If people could only see Him, what He endured for us, then surely their hearts would be touched."

Suffering, she believes, is a gift.

"The Gospa has told us this – that it is a gift and that we should receive it as a gift.

"But there is a difference in our suffering. There is the suffering that God gives us when we leave ourselves open to His will and offer our sufferings for His intentions. And then there is the suffering that we search for in our lives."

Vicka herself has suffered greatly from sickness over the years, but now, as in the earlier years when she was rigorously questioned about it, she prefers not to discuss the subject.

Some have said that this is physical suffering, I remark, others that it is spiritual.

"It is physical suffering," she says with finality, when pressed.

"Our Lady wanted it that way. And it was for Our Lady's special intentions."

Now, as when the suffering first began in 1984, Vicka refuses to talk about it. It is known, however, that it began with severe headaches and fainting, and developed into regular coma-like periods, severe pain and, at times, vomiting. No amount of medical tests, agreed to by Vicka because of the concern of her family and carried out in various hospitals, could identify the exact cause. But over time, it became obvious to those around her that Vicka had agreed to enter into this suffering, for love of the Gospa and for the fulfilment of Her intentions.

It was also obvious that she had made an agreement not to speak of it.

Once, over a year after the suffering began, Vicka's mother, distressed by the deterioration in her daughter's health and the continuance of the coma-like episodes, begged Vicka to ask the Virgin Mary to relieve her of her misery, even a little. Vicka's response was immediate. "Oh, Mama. If you only knew how many souls are helped by this, you would not ask me that."

And throughout these often intense periods of pain and illness, Vicka continued to live life as normally as possible, meeting with huge crowds of pilgrims each day despite being so ill and weak at times that she could barely stand, begging the Virgin to give her just enough strength to carry out this duty of love. And even, during one period, climbing Križevac on her own for fifty consecutive days in what her family could only believe was in special response to the Gospa's request.

Twice also, during the early days of this suffering,

Vicka accepted the Gospa's decision for long interruptions to the daily apparitions, silently enduring the sadness of not meeting with her Heavenly Mother, and showing incredible joy when the apparitions began again.

So many of those who come to Medjugorje are ill, I now observe.

Much of the time I'd spent here was waiting for Vicka, who spends long hours every day meeting with and praying for the sick.

It is something that Our Lady has asked of her, she replies simply.

"Mirjana prays for those who do not yet know the love of God. I pray for the sick. Each one of us prays for a special intention of Our Lady.

"Almost every person who comes here is sick," she continues.

"Either they are sick in a physical or in a spiritual way. I rarely meet people who are healthy. But when they come with their families, I unite them together in prayer, which is the best way to allow Jesus to work in our lives."

A priest once said here in Medjugorje, I recall, that all physical healings were simply an aid to spiritual healing.

"Of course", she agrees.

"I believe that God does it in that way. He sees the need that we have and He works in that way. Our Lady says that many times we pray only for the physical healing and we don't do anything else to change our lives. We neglect the spiritual side of our beings and only through spiritual change can real healing come.

"We ask all the time and Our Lady says that she is very happy when we ask, but she is also very happy when we give, because if we give more then we will have more courage to ask. But if we don't give, then that is just selfishness."

The anguish of those who come in search of physical healing is enormous, I observe – especially those who bring their sick in the hope of a miracle.

"We are all just people – this is very human," Vicka says, her own personal experience of suffering giving her an insight beyond that of many others.

"But the most important thing is our spiritual healing.

"And because we are human, we find suffering very difficult.

"Our Lady sometimes says that if God gives us suffering, then that is a great gift from Him.

"When that suffering comes, most of us say 'Why God, why me?' and we all want to rid ourselves of the suffering.

"But Our Lady says that when we receive this gift of suffering we should say, 'Dear God, thank you for this gift. But please, give me the strength to deal with it'.

"And she also says we should not think that God does not recognise our suffering. She says, 'You cannot even imagine how big your suffering is in God's eyes'."

"Dear Children," the Gospa said in her message of 11 September 1986.

"For these days, while you are joyfully celebrating the cross, I desire that your cross also would be a joy for you. Especially, dear children, pray that you may be able to accept sickness and suffering with love, the way Jesus accepted them. Only that way shall I be able with joy to give out to you the graces and healings which Jesus is permitting me. Thank you for having responded to my call."

To accept suffering with love is something almost alien to the human side of our being. It remains a mystery 'even when we meditate upon it in front of Our Lord's Cross' wrote Fr. Slavko Barbarić in his book *In the School of Love*.

"Illness and suffering are crosses which can easily close the human heart to God. We ask, 'Why, O God?' However, it is generally true that the experience of personal or family suffering usually brings fruits of faith, love and hope."

And, he continues, in the same vein as Vicka, Our Lady tells us how we can cope with our crosses.

"She does not say 'Carry your cross' because she knows that we are weak. Instead she said, 'Pray that you can accept illness and suffering with love'.

"We usually pray that the Lord lifts our suffering and crosses, and this is understandable. But we have to accept the fact that we need to pray to be able to accept our crosses and suffering with love."

The message that Vicka Ivanković, who herself has endured much suffering, would give to the sick and to those who find their burdens heavy is simple, direct, but heartfelt.

"I would recommend that, with patience, they would try to carry the gift of their cross.

"Every night, when Our Lady appears to me, I first recommend all the sick people, and then everybody else.

"And I know that Our Lady gives special help and comfort to those who are sick and who ask for her intercession with her Son."

The suffering of families is also especially close to the heart of the Gospa?

"That is true," Vicka responds. "And she asks that especially we pray for young people in the family because they are in a very very difficult situation.

"Drugs, divorce, everything that is bad in the world – these are all the things that are attacking families. And that attack becomes stronger every day, Our Lady says, because the windows and the doors of our homes are open to Satan, and we don't do anything to defend ourselves.

"Our Lady says that Satan uses every free moment for himself – and he does this most of all on the young people of today because he wants to destroy our families.

"Families are not so close any more. Everybody does their own thing and people are not close to each other. Everything else is more important than our being together. But until we receive Jesus back into our families, Our Lady says, so that He becomes the centre of our lives and that with Him we can live together and find more time for each other, none of this will change.

"That is why Our Lady emphasizes so often that we begin again to pray in the family, to pray the rosary together. 'With prayer and fasting', she says, 'you can stop wars'. That is how strong these weapons are.

"With prayer and fasting, we can change our families, defend our children. She has told us this. But now it is up to us to decide will we receive this message from her and live it."

Again, my memory is drawn to what a retired Archbishop had to say on his August 1995 visit to Medjugorje. The renowned exorcist had no difficulties in accepting the destructive influences of Satan in our world. A great deal of his work during his career had been with the possessed and with people under Satan's influence.

According to what he had seen in his work as a priest over twenty-three years, he said, "I think that Satan tries mostly to destroy families.

"I know that some Satanic sects exist with the sole

purpose of fasting for the breakdown of families. In the world, there are various Satanic organisations which try to destroy individuals and families."

The fact is, he continued, that so many families are in danger because of a lack of faith, because of alcoholism and because of divorce.

"This all leads to a breakdown of family life."

The way to fight against this, he said, was with prayer and fasting.

"There already exist exorcism prayers, which the priests pray, but everybody can help to free people from the influence of Satan. We must call on the name of Jesus, the intercession of the saints, especially the Blessed Virgin Mary. It's important to pray the rosary."

And for those who fear evil, the Archbishop had a special message.

"Nobody should be afraid, or think that they are possessed. Priests must strengthen the faithful in their confidence in the battle against Satan. We must teach the people to praise God the Father, the Holy Spirit and to venerate the Blessed Virgin, Our Mother, Mary. We must teach the people to live the Sacraments and that there is no reason to fear. But rather, we must pray and love."

"Dear Children," the Gospa said on 25 September 1991.

"Today in a special way I invite you all to prayer and renunciation. For now, as never before, Satan wants to show the world his shameful face by which he wants to seduce as many people as possible onto the way of death and sin. Therefore, dear children, help my Immaculate Heart to triumph in the sinful world. I beseech all of you to offer prayers and sacrifices for my intentions, so I can present them to God for what is most

necessary. Forget your desires, dear children, and pray for what God desires, and not for what you desire. Thank you for having responded to my call."

Chapter 4

A new beginning

Goran Čukević – Čuke to all who knew him – woke with a start. He'd been dreaming: terrible dreams of untold horrors that left him gasping and choking as he tried to drag his mind back to reality.

Looking around him, he thought for a moment that he was still locked in the dream. Lying on a piece of cardboard in the middle of winter in a derelict building with no windows or doors, his surroundings were the stuff of nightmares.

But he wasn't asleep.

This was reality, all right. His reality. And as the horror finally ate into his fuddled brain, he began to cry.

Thirty years of age and he had nothing and nobody. No family, no friends, not even a plate for his food, if he had any food. Nothing . . . nothing . . . nothing.

He'd tried to kill himself again. Two, three days ago – whatever it was. He'd taken a box of tablets and a bottle of vodka and some heroin, and after that he must have fallen into some sort of coma.

But, like all the other times, he'd woken up again. Like when he'd cut his veins a while back. Somebody had always appeared to patch him up, put him out on the streets again.

He didn't think he could stand much more of it.

As the tears poured down his face, making tracks in the dirt and grime, Čuke – in total desperation – turned to the one person he had never asked for help. And started to pray.

"Hail Mary, holy Mary," he wept, "pray for us."

It was coming out all wrong. He couldn't even remember this properly.

"Please, Our Lady," he sobbed, "either take me to you so that I finish this miserable life. Or else show me the road to get out of all this."

Had it always been this way? Painfully, his broken mind tried to retrace the stumbling steps of his life.

He'd been born in Split, the beautiful Croatian city on the Adriatic coast, thirty years before.

"I was born into a Catholic family," he says now, almost seven years later, in his partly built home on the outskirts of Medjugorje.

"But Catholicism was really just a tradition which went down from generation to generation. When I was growing up under a communist regime, I did what I was supposed to do to show that you were against communism. I went to my catechism lessons. I was even an altar boy. But that was all because I was made do it. I was sent to Mass, although neither my father nor mother nor brother went. Faith, to me, meant that at Christmas and Easter you did what the others did – you roasted a lamb, you spent a bit of money and that was that."

Tragedy had already hit the Čukević household. When she was only four years old, his younger sister fell out of the fourth floor window and was killed. His younger brother contracted meningitis when he was just one year old and was left deaf and dumb. His father, who was a sailor at the time, was more often away from home. And in the midst of all this, Čuke's mother was diagnosed with leukaemia.

Early on in his life, Čuke says, he learned to avoid the difficulties of family life by seeking the company of friends. "When I was six years old, I robbed my first bar of chocolate. And automatically, when I did this, I had to tell my first real lie."

By the age of seven or eight, he had begun to steal bits of money from his mother's purse. As her illness worsened and her grief for her dead daughter was mingled with worry for her wild young son, she began to suffer from depression.

"It was true that I loved her, but it was difficult to live in that house and look at that depression. And she spent an awful lot of time just sitting there in front of the television. So at the age of eleven, I began to drink alcohol and smoke cigarettes. It wasn't even that I liked them, in fact I thought that they were disgusting, but with alcohol and cigarettes I felt like a man.

"And all my heroes – those television and film idols – were hard and mean and had tattoos on their bodies, or scars all over their faces. And I wanted to be like them because I felt that that's what it took to be a man.

"If you were a real man, then you wouldn't be good. Goodness was for women."

His friends were always older, he recalls, never his own age. And they encouraged him to take alcohol.

"When I drank, I was able to rob a car – I was able to do things I would normally never be able to do."

His mother died when he was thirteen. Despite his tough front, Čuke took her death badly.

"All that next year, until I was fourteen, I kept saying how I was going to kill myself. And everybody thought – he's just saying that, it will pass.

"But on the first anniversary of her death I took a pistol

and I shot myself in the head.

"It's twenty-three years now since I put that bullet in my head and it's still there. It lodged somewhere and they said it would be too dangerous to remove."

From there, he says, it was all downhill. He became depressed. Alcohol was easily available to him and he began to take more and more.

One day somebody came to him and said 'Look, marijuana is even better than alcohol'. He was bored of alcohol. Tired of always being sick after drinking too much. So he lit his first joint – and liked it.

"First of all, I limited myself to one at the weekend. I thought I was in control. Then it became two during the week and then three. And then it became every day. Alcohol and tablets were always there too. And every day I grew further away from reality. I realised that I was beginning to lose control. I began to forget things. I began to curse. And I began to fall more and more into paranoia and depression.

"So I decided not to smoke it any more. But I needed something to exchange it with – and that's when heroin came into my life."

In the meantime, he recalls, his father decided to remarry and his stepmother came into the home.

"I hated her. Why, I don't know, because she really did bring light into the house. She was a devout woman and she brought prayer into the house, but the more she prayed the more I hated her."

It was the heroin, he says, that 'opened the doors of hell' for him.

About two and a half years after he began to take drugs, his father discovered the rubber which Čuke used to make his veins pop out.

"My father's world crumbled around him. He couldn't escape from the problem he now saw before him. He had to identify with the truth and that was very hard for him.

"So he tried to talk to me and that did nothing. And then he tried to come into my world, but we were too alike and we both flared up. And in those moments, when he got mad, he would beat me to bits.

"Finally, he realised that while I was on heroin there was no point in beating me any more because I was completely out of my mind. I was crazy. So he tried to talk to me, to extend some sort of love towards me, but there was a wall between us.

"When that didn't work, he resorted to psychiatry. But I came out of three months of psychiatry worse than when I went in, because regularly my friends would come to visit me in the psychiatric unit of Split Hospital and would bring drugs to me."

During that time, Čuke says, he had a girlfriend. Even now, he finds it hard to believe what it was in him that made him treat her the way he did.

"I thought I loved her. And in one sense I did. But when I had to choose between heroin and Zeljka, I chose heroin. She started to take it with me.

"I came out of the psychiatric unit and was no better than when I'd gone in, so my father decided to allow me to be put in jail. He thought jail might knock some sense into me. But what can you learn in jail except what's a better way to steal, what's a better way to get a car, what's a better way to be dishonest? And the minute I got out of jail, I continued on the same road."

His father found him a job in the warehouse of the company in which he worked.

"I stole half of the stuff there, borrowed money from all

43

his friends and never gave it back, and made my father really ashamed of me.

"My girlfriend, in the meantime, became pregnant. When she was three months' pregnant, she wanted us to stop the way of life we were living and start on the right road.

"So I decided that she should abort the baby.

"She didn't want to, but I made her. You can imagine how bad I was by this time. She got the money together and gave it to me so that I could pay the doctor. But I sent her in there and then I ran off with the money."

Back at home, the family was disintegrating.

"If it had just been heroin, it would have been bad enough, but I always mixed it with alcohol", Čuke says, his eyes full of pain as he looks back at that person in what now seems another life.

"So one day, I got out of jail once again and found the door closed on me. My father said, 'Look son, you've the right to destroy yourself and I can't stop you. But you don't have the right to destroy the rest of us. You go out there, you take as many drugs as you want to, drink yourself to death if you want to, but don't come back here while you're doing it. Only if you decide to be a man can you come back to this home and then I'll help you'.

"At that moment, I hated him. I hated the whole world – everybody – because I thought that everybody else was guilty because I had arrived at this point."

God didn't even come into the picture, he says.

"I never even remembered Him. Often, I was selling and dealing drugs around churches and I'd see people going in and I would shout at them and insult them. The only time I went into a church was to take the money from the box."

He was almost nine years living on the streets, he says.

"And that little bit of dignity, that little bit of love, or character, that I might have had – I lost even that. Because I never believed that there were such things as good people in the world. Every one of them was corrupt, I believed. And that's the way I behaved towards them.

"I would break into houses and apartments twenty-four hours a day. I would threaten people and hold them up. Many a time I was put in jail. And when I got out of jail I was worse than before.

"In the end, I had twenty-seven crimes to my name. So the social services, the police department, the Department of Justice and everybody else decided to get together. They decided not to send me to jail any more. They'd send me to the asylum instead."

He was two and a half years in a criminal asylum, where he was surrounded by murderers and others who had committed some of the most horrible crimes imaginable.

"These were people with pathological tendencies. They liked to kill. And most of the time, I was afraid there.

"But when I think back, I was afraid my whole life through, but I learned to overcome that fear with aggressiveness. I wanted others to be afraid of me, so that they wouldn't know how much I was afraid of them."

He reached the stage, however, where he could no longer cope with the asylum and the terrible fear every day brought.

"I managed to steal 50 Deutchmarks off a man who had murdered four people – and then I made my escape."

He was on the run for about a month before the police recaptured him and sent him back to the asylum. Even today, the sweat visibly gleams on his forehead as he remembers the horror that followed.

"As soon as they got me back into the hospital, the doctor got me into a room and beat me almost senseless. I remember him driving his fist into my stomach and saying, 'I am God here. I can do what I want. I can kill you if I want'. And things were even worse because it was wartime. There was nobody to turn to.

"And then, so that they could completely destroy me, they put me into the room with that same man I had stolen the 50 marks from. The one who had murdered four people! They put me into a strait-jacket and they tied my legs to the bed, and the only time they untied me was occasionally to go to the toilet when they would take me out, wipe my backside and put me back into the room.

"For seven days that man just sat there, smoking cigarettes and staring at me. He never said a word. And every time he got up, I wet myself with fear because I couldn't do anything – I couldn't even defend myself. And I knew that plenty of times, within that asylum, murders took place."

After a week of sheer terror, during which Čuke only slept in fits and starts when total exhaustion overtook him, the other man suddenly began to speak.

"He cursed me. He cursed my mother and all my family. He said, 'You s…, you know who I am and you know what I've done and you know what I can do. And you still stole money from me. But if you have the b…. to do that, I congratulate you'.

"And with that he stuck a cigarette into my mouth and lit it. And every time I needed to go to the toilet after that he would bring me, and all day he would stick cigarettes into my mouth."

Many of Čuke's teeth and most of his hair had fallen out before he was finally released from the asylum. The night before he was to leave, he was so frightened of the outside world that he got a razor and cut his veins. They patched him up and next morning set him free.

He didn't know where to go.

Back in Split, he started taking drugs again. His weight was down to less than fifty kilos and he could barely walk. He had lost the habit of sleeping, his mind was destroyed and he hadn't eaten for seven or eight days.

At rock bottom, he begged the dealers he knew to give him drugs. Without money, they refused. His strength was gone. Too weak even to break into houses, he was shunned by the other addicts on the city's streets. Nobody wanted to be with him.

That night, he crawled through the broken window of a derelict house, lay down on a piece of cardboard and finally dropped off to sleep – until the nightmares wakened him and left him crying and pleading for help from the Mother of God.

Every morning, for four days, he recalls, he awoke on the freezing floor and cried and prayed for help.

On the fourth day, completely weakened and broken, he managed to drag himself away from the house and found his way into a park nearby.

It was about 7 or 8 in the morning, he believes. He sat there, shivering and freezing and ill, watching people come and go from a church close by.

"All I could think was 'What will I do, what will I do, what will I do . . .', over and over again."

The words of the Hail Mary, as he again tried to say them, remained jumbled in his mind. Nothing was clear any longer.

"And then I saw this woman and she was coming straight towards me. I was looking at her and thinking she will turn that way or that way, but she kept coming straight towards me.

"I didn't know what to do. I was afraid that once I had robbed something from her and now she was looking for revenge, but I didn't have the strength to run away.

"And then she came up to me and said good morning, and I stared at her and said good morning in return. And she said to me, 'Listen, young fellow, I have a problem'. And I interrupted her and said, 'Look, missus, leave me alone. I have more problems than you can even think of'.

"But she kept on talking. And she said, 'I'm looking for a young fellow. His name is Čuke. I know that he hangs around here somewhere. Would you be able to help me find him?'

"I didn't know what to do. If I said that was me, maybe she would start screaming. And then I'd have to hit her and try to run. But I found myself saying, 'That's me – I'm Čuke'. And the lady started to cry.

"I thought 'That's it, she's crazy'. But then she took me by the arm and said, 'Please, come for a walk with me'. And I said okay.

"But before we moved away she said, 'Please, just take the stuff out of your pockets and throw it away – the rubbers, the syringes, the spoon'. All that stuff was everything to me. I needed it to take heroin.

"But I listened to her and I don't know why, because I had never listened to anybody in my life. And she started to talk to me.

"She was the mother of a guy that I knew – not a friend, just somebody I knew on the streets, and he had ended up in jail. She, like any mother, went to see her son in jail. And it's very strange, all this, because usually people who are drug addicts are very selfish and only ever think of themselves.

"So I don't know why, but every time his mother went to see him, this guy would mention me. He would say, 'Please, somebody has to do something for Čuke. He's going to kill himself. Somebody has to find him'."

Desperate to help her son, the woman finally managed to get him out of jail and into the Cenacalo community in Medjugorje.

"She then went looking for me and she found me, walked right up to me, and then she set about finding documents for me – identification card and all those things that I hadn't used for years. And at times I would run away from her, and then when I had no drugs I would go back looking for her again. And despite how dirty I was and the smell – I hadn't had a bath in four or five years – she took me home to her house.

"Then one day she came to me with a bus ticket. She took me to a bus and gave the ticket to the driver and told him I wasn't to get off until I was in Medjugorje.

"And she told me that Our Lady was appearing there."

It was the beginning of a long and hard journey for Čuke, not just to a valley in Herzegovina, but back to life.

He admits that at the time, he never really thought that he could ever get himself away from drugs.

"Nor was I conscious that Our Lady was holding out her hands to me. I went to Medjugorje and to Cenacalo because I heard that the community had beds. And that there would be something to eat there. And I wouldn't be alone. And I thought – you know what? I'll go up there and stay until winter is over and then I'll go back down to Split because I didn't think that there was any way out of drugs for me."

When they saw the pitiful state he was in, Sr. Elvira and the Cenacalo community immediately took Čuke in. It was a new beginning.

"But that beginning in Cenacalo was harder for me than all the years I had spent on the streets," he says now.

"It was hard for me because it came to the point where I had to start seeing my reflection in the mirror. And I had to start realising and admitting to myself that I'm the one who made the mistakes.

"I didn't know who I was. I had even forgotten how to talk properly. My whole vocabulary had turned into the curses I'd learned on the streets.

"And so, when I arrived up there, I had to start fighting against myself. I had to begin sorting out all that rubbish that was inside me.

"It was hard – very hard – at the age of thirty to try to create a new character."

It was a long and painful road. Čuke wanted to be alone as he tried to work things out in his head. The Cenacalo policy ruled this out. Always, he was shadowed by what the community called his 'guardian angel', a former addict who had already walked the difficult path to recovery.

Čuke was afraid of everything. Afraid of showing weakness. Afraid of being alone. Afraid of being with others. Afraid of living without drugs. Afraid to look closely at himself. Afraid to pray.

"I could speak of a hundred different incidents," he says quietly, "but in short those boys up there and Sr. Elvira – from day to day they started to build me up, they started to give me strength.

"I began to change – little things inside me, but at the beginning I didn't see many fruits. And then I started to be jealous because other boys' parents came to visit them and nobody ever came to visit me.

"And I began to think how much I'd love to see my

Dad, to say sorry to him. And the other boys said to me, 'If you really want to see your family, get up at two in the morning and get down on your knees in the chapel and pray'. And I got up and I prayed, but I didn't really believe.

"Then one day, about two weeks later, Sr. Elvira decided that I should learn to make icons because she knew that this would purify me. I was doing this when some guy called me and said, 'Come on, Čuke, there's a group here from Split. Why don't you lead them around the camp and explain a little about the way we live?'

"And I said okay, no problem.

"I came to the living room and opened the door – and I saw my father!"

At that moment, all he wanted to do was to run away, Čuke says. And then he thought – where would he go? All of his life he'd been running.

"But I was so embarrassed and ashamed because of all the ill that I had done to him. I didn't have the strength to look him in the face and I put my head down and looked up just a little at him.

"And what would a father do? He got up and he held out his hand to me and he started to cry. And I started to cry and then we began to hug and kiss each other.

"The whole day we just walked around the community, both of us crying. And that evening when he was leaving, I said, 'Look, I'm going to try to stay here in this community and take all the bad that I did and try to pay it back three times over in goodness."

The days passed into months. Three years and eight months – during which time he also helped to found a Cenacalo community in Italy – before he felt capable of leaving and moving on with his life. During this time, he made peace with himself, with the world and with the God he'd come to know as he lived and worked under the mantle of the Gospa.

The Franciscans helped him when he finally left the community, by offering him work in the parish. His first job was cleaning the public toilets in Medjugorje. After that he was 'promoted' – he got a broom in his hand and swept around the church.

Still later, he sanded down and varnished the hundreds of wooden benches both inside and outside the church. But the heavy work took its toll on his abused body: he ended up with back problems and had to undergo surgery.

Afterwards, the Franciscan priests took him into the parish office, where he handled the money that came in from the collections. Their trust in him did more, he says, than almost anything else to fully heal him.

More than anything, however, he longed for one more thing – for a girl to share both his life and the huge untapped wealth of love stored up inside him. It was a dream that seemed impossible to realise.

"Who would want me when you take into consideration my past? Who would entrust their daughter to me?"

He suffered – and he prayed.

"I really prayed. And then one day Katarina came.

"For me, Katarina could only have been some sort of dream. She had no big stains on her past life, she was beautiful and thirteen years younger than me and had always been faithful to the church."

Over eight months, he fell more and more in love with her from afar. And when she came to know him and to see the goodness in him as he worked with the orphaned children and the old people in the parish, Katarina, who had come from the Czech Republic to stay in Medjugorje, fell in love with him, too.

They married and his father sold a small apartment he owned and shared the money with Čuke and his brother. The money allowed Čuke to begin building a home of his own, on the outskirts of Medjugorje.

At present it's a shell, only partly finished, and Čuke and Katarina never know where their next meal is coming from. It's a worry sometimes, particularly now that their baby daughter is born, and often there is nothing to eat.

"But that's when God sends somebody to us and for another day we manage," Čuke says.

In his spare time, he makes beautiful icons – a long and costly process that he learned in Cenacalo, but which, when he finds somebody willing to purchase, helps keep the family going.

He's working also on a drug rehabilitation project in Mostar. Fr. Slavko Barbarić had recommended Čuke when asked by the Centre's director.

"Are you sure I can trust this man?" the doctor had asked. "Trust him?" Fr. Slavko replied. "I would entrust the whole of Mostar to him."

It was a recommendation that remains very dear to Čuke who, like so many others in Medjugorje, dearly loved this Franciscan priest and misses him greatly since his death in November 2000.

The wage he receives at the drug centre is minimal, but the satisfaction of helping another fellow human off the treadmill of drugs and crime is well worth the long hours and huge effort.

"The solution, you see, is not just to stop taking heroin," Čuke says with feeling. "It can only come from changing yourself, by turning to God and putting Him in the first place in your life. That's what I learned in Cenacalo."

"*Dear Children,*" the Gospa said in Medjugorje on 25 March 1996.

"*I invite you to decide again to love God above all else. In this time, when due to the spirit of consumerism one forgets what it means to love and to cherish true values, I invite you again, little children, to put God in the first place in your life. Do not let Satan attract you through material things but, little children, decide for God who is freedom and love. Choose life and not death of the soul, little children, and in this time when you meditate upon the suffering and death of Jesus, I invite you to decide for life which blossomed through the Resurrection, and that your life may be renewed today through conversion that shall lead you to eternal life. Thank you for having responded to my call.*"

Chapter 5

Healing the wounded

You spend a great deal of time in the Cenacalo community here in Medjugorje, I observe to Vicka, as the morning draws on and the sounds of village life filter into the quiet room.

"Yes, what time I can," she replies with a warm smile, tidying up a sheaf of prayer requests that were given to her earlier by a group leader, with the plea that they be recommended to the Virgin at that evening's apparition.

"I was there a lot when Sr. Elvira first founded the community and I became good friends with her on a personal basis, and then with those in the community. It is a great gift to be with people who are searching for something, trying to find themselves, who are in the darkness but searching for the light.

"They are special people, they help each other through all the pain of change and are such good friends that they would do anything for each other.

"This is the basis on which the Cenacalo communities flourish – to use the love and prayer of the whole community to heal one another."

A community was opened in Ireland in recent years, I tell her, and has already touched the lives of many who had thought they could never be happy or whole again.

"Yes, there are now thirty-six houses all over the world," she replies with a smile full of happiness.

"They are just now opening a new house in Russia and

there is a great need for all of these. But they must first have people in each country whose hearts are open and who are willing to open a new house, and then they will find that there are volunteers in all of the other houses who are willing to go to these countries and put down the foundations for a new community, to help change the lives of addicts.

"After this, it is possible for others to come into this house and experience the special thing that is Cenacalo."

Vicka's love and admiration for Sr. Elvira is mirrored not only in the young men and women who found God's love and healing within the community, but by thousands of others whose lives they have touched.

Born Rita Agnes Petrozzi, the fourth child of seven in an ordinary Italian family, Sr. Elvira learned from an early age how to care for others. During World War II, with her father away on military service and her mother working in a local hospital, she became the central figure in the family, caring for the home and her brothers and sisters, even those older than herself.

Serving others became part of her nature and it was no surprise to all who knew her when she decided, at the age of nineteen, to enter the community of the Sisters of Love, founded by St. Joan Antida. There, she took her vow to serve the poor and gained the name she is known by today – Elvira, which means 'strong woman'.

She spent twenty-five years there, happily serving in all areas of the Order's life, but deep inside was a voice urging her on.

"Something within continuously urged me to dedicate myself to the poor of our times, especially to the young addicts, because they are our poorest contemporaries, with no family, no security, no feeling of self-worth and no respect for others. They are the rejected ones."

Her request to dedicate herself entirely to this work was rejected by her superiors eleven times over six years. But Elvira, the 'strong woman', waited patiently, convinced that if it were the will of God her request would be answered in time. Finally, in 1983, when she was forty-six years old, the permission came and she opened the first community house for addicts in Saluzzo, near Turin, Italy.

Her potent combination of deep true love for God and all others, prayer and the reading of the Holy Scriptures, of hard work and the support of others on the same road, has worked miracles in the lives of thousands.

Her love for others in pain and need began back in her own family and childhood, she believes. Her father was an alcoholic, to the extent that even as a child she often felt ashamed and humiliated as she left her home to go and search for him in neighbours' homes. And yet, she says, it was many years later, standing by his deathbed, that she thanked God for such a father because had he not been what he was, she herself would probably never have developed such a great love and affection for all other addicts.

Neither doctors nor psychiatrists play any part in the rehabilitation of the people who come to her community, which was based on 'cenacles' rather than hospital wards. Recognising in the desperate illness of addiction the absence of God, Sr. Elvira uses His loving presence as the only medication that could heal these empty, wounded and abandoned hearts.

In 1985, two years after founding the first Cenacolo community, she came to Medjugorje for the first time, her curiosity aroused both by what she had read of the events there and by the testimonies and spiritual experiences of others. She brought with her some of those already living in the Italian community.

Shortly after arriving, she met with the visionaries Vicka and Marija. Their openness and the profound spiritual effect the apparitions had had on their lives made a deep impression on Sr. Elvira.

The following year, she returned with another group – this time for forty days – and the year after that for six months. Before long, she had founded a new community in the Medjugorje hamlet of Bijakovići, placing all in its care under the protection of the Mother of God.

"Each addict", she once said, "is a wonderful pearl that has fallen into a swamp and it is enough to take it in the hand, to polish it, so that it shines again."

And every morning, I am reminded, as I sit here in this quiet room with Vicka, that the boys in the Cenacalo community in Medjugorje, as in all their other community houses across Europe, say the same prayer of love and commitment:

"In awareness of my Christian mission, I _____ put my baptismal pledge into your hands, Mary. I withstand Satan, I withstand drugs, I withstand all evil, all his temptation and all his works, and I consecrate myself to Jesus Christ to faithfully carry my cross with Him each day, according to the will of God. In the presence of the Church I accept you, Mary, as my Mother and Empress. I consecrate to you my person, my life and the value of all my good deeds: the past, the present and the future. Direct me, and everything that belongs to me, to the greater glory of God for all time and in all eternity. Amen."

Chapter 6

Her beloved sons

"Dear Children," the Gospa said on 25 November 2000.

"Today, when heaven is near to you in a special way, I call you to prayer so that through prayer you place God in the first place. Little children, today I am near you and I bless each of you with my motherly blessing so that you have the strength and love for all the people you meet in your earthly life, and that you can give God's love. I rejoice with you and I desire to tell you that your brother Slavko has been born into Heaven and intercedes for you. Thank you for having responded to my call."

The sudden and untimely death on 24 November 2000 of Fr. Slavko Barbarić, the Franciscan priest who through his deep spirituality had become for millions worldwide inexorably linked with the prayerful fruits of Medjugorje, had a profound effect on all who heard the news.

From being first sent to Medjugorje in 1982 to sound out the theological claims of the phenomena, he developed a deep personal belief in the reported apparitions. Born in Dragicina, Herzegovina, in 1946, he was ordained a priest in 1971. With his degrees in Pastoral Theology and Psychotherapy, and a doctorate in Religious Pedagogy, he was uniquely equipped to investigate the happenings in the valley.

Over the coming years, he worked tirelessly in the parish and was instrumental in developing a strong spiritual and pastoral programme that allowed both the native parishioners and over twenty million pilgrims to grow in the love of Jesus and under the protection of His Mother Mary in this unique school of prayer.

His death at 3.30 in the afternoon, just below the peak of Mount Križevac – having led the parish in prayer up the steep mountain in their regular Friday Stations of the Cross – sent shock waves of loss right across the world.

"We knew something terrible had happened when you did not come to visit us on Friday evening as you promised you would," one of the orphans from the Mother's Village, which Fr. Slavko had built, said in a voice choked with tears at the funeral. And all over Medjugorje, children wept for the priest they had laughed and played and prayed with.

"How could we not remember each of your sacrifices and each of your battles for us," said Jakov Čolo, speaking at the graveside on behalf of all six visionaries.

"How could we not remember your goodness and your love for us.

"You often said to us, 'Do you know that I love you?'

"We felt that love so often and in so many different ways.

"Often, after the apparition, you would ask us, 'How is Our Lady?' You, dear brother, are now with Her. You, who consecrated your life to Her. You, who did everything for everyone to come to know Her love and Her goodness.

"That love and goodness were actually in you and this could be experienced by every person who came to know you."

And when, a year later, a stone memorial, weighing 950 kg, was erected on the spot where he gave his soul into the hands of his Lord, it took nine hours to be carried up the steep rocky path in the arms of the boys from the

Cenacalo community. As they climbed, thousands of friends, family, parishioners and foreign pilgrims prayed and meditated on that love that gives itself without reserve, just as was demonstrated by this much-loved priest.

But just as so many in Medjugorje and right across the world struggled to come to terms with their pain and loss, the Virgin's message (given as usual on the 25th of each month) contained the Franciscan's name, on the very day after his death. The Gospa said, *"I rejoice with you and I desire to tell you that your brother Slavko has been born into Heaven and intercedes for you"*.

Never before, in the nineteen years of her reported and much investigated apparitions in the valley of Medjugorje, had the Queen of Peace given such news about any individual.

Vicka Ivanković shows no sign of sadness at the mention of the priest's name.

As a deep warm smile lights up first her eyes and then her whole face, I am reminded of how, I was told, while all others wept openly on the evening of Fr. Slavko's death, Vicka, on coming to pay her respects in the Chapel of Adoration where his body was laid out, smiled happily as she gazed down on the priest who had been her friend and counsellor, before moving to comfort his broken-hearted mother.

"I think that his death was a gift," she says simply, "and that God has given a very great grace to him.

"Yes, his loss affected we visionaries a lot, but we are very thankful to God that we had a person like that, who was a wonderful role model that we could follow."

The love of the Gospa for priests – 'my beloved sons' –

has been well documented through the testimonies of all six visionaries over the years.

On 13 October 1984, over two hundred priests were gathered in Medjugorje. As there were too many to fit into the tiny chapel off the altar, where the Gospa was then appearing to the visionaries before evening Mass each day, Fr. Tomislav Vlašić invited the priests to the basement of the rectory instead. There, they were joined by the visionaries. During the apparition, the Virgin gave a message especially for them, through Marija Pavlović:

"My very dear sons," she said. *"Today, my son Jesus has allowed me to bring you together here, to give this message to you and to all those who love me. My very dear sons, pray constantly and ask the Holy Spirit to inspire you always. In all your requests and in all your actions, have only one desire, to accomplish basically the holy will of God. My very dear sons, thank you for having answered my call."*

Fr. Vlašić added his own words of encouragement briefly to that – "Deepen your faith, pray constantly, fast, receive the Sacrament of Reconciliation: these are the requests of the Blessed Virgin Mary."

What is the most important message Our Lady has for priests, I ask Vicka.

"She says that priests should keep the faith of their people and they should preach the Gospel and they should pray the Rosary with their people," she replies without hesitation.

"Our Lady said, too, that some priests respond better to the call of their vocation and to their care of the people, and we should help all priests with our prayers, so that God will give them the grace and strength they need to believe fully in Him and to bring Him to His people, especially through the Sacrament of Confession and through His presence in the Holy Eucharist.

"And she said that we should pray especially for the newly ordained priests, and for vocations, because there are not enough priests to carry out the work of her Son."

For a few moments she is silent, her eyes on the crucifix on the wall. Then she turns back to me, her face more serious than I have seen it before.

"Our Lady has especially told us that we should tell all the people to pray for our Holy Father the Pope, to pray for our bishops, our priests – the entire church. Our priests are in great need of our prayers, she has said."

It's a message that Vicka has not been slow to give over the years, as the Gospa continuously called on the faithful to support and pray for their priests.

And the fruits of Medjugorje, in the renewal of the gifts of faith, have not been restricted to the laity.

In November 1997, during his visit to Medjugorje, Bishop Lazaro Perez from Mexico spoke about his impressions and about his meeting with Vicka.

"This morning we talked with a visionary, Vicka," he said. "She presented to us Our Lady's messages on conversion, fasting, prayer, forgiveness and holy confession, about all these values that are gradually being lost today.

"I personally believe the following: If Our Lady through Christ is endeavouring to quicken these values, then that ought to be the fundamental duty of a priest, especially of us bishops. We have to tell the faithful that this world has a way of salvation, because Christ is our way. Christ is our Saviour and here we see that the Mother of

Christ calls us to this – to enliven the values that lead to salvation. These are prayer, reconciliation, conversion and fasting, in such a way that we can be closer to the cross of Christ."

In mid-May of 1997, Bishop Frederick Drandua from Uganda spoke of his own personal experience of renewal during his week-long visit to the parish of Medjugorje.

"People come and change their lives," he observed.

"Many confess. In these last ten years as a bishop, I hardly ever heard confessions. Here, people were constantly asking me to hear their confessions and I did. In these days, I must have heard over one hundred confessions.

"I'm certain that the Lord is using this place for the conversion of nations. On my return home, I intend to preach about the rosary and I will recommend to priests that they dedicate one day in the week to Adoration."

Archbishop Frane Franić, retired Archbishop of Split-Makarska, Croatia, a deeply Spirit-filled priest who has made widely known his personal and highly supportive views of the happenings at Medjugorje, spoke movingly in the same vein at the Mass to celebrate his Diamond Jubilee in December 1996.

In the packed cathedral in Split and in front of the Papal Nuncio, Giulio Einaudi, Croatian Cardinal Franjo Kuharić, and his own successor as Archbishop, Monsignor Ante Jurić, Archbishop Franić once again did not hesitate to voice his personal belief in the challenge of Mary for today's priests.

"Every priest should pray three hours a day and every bishop, four. Every retired bishop should pray five hours a day," he told the congregation. "I personally learned how to pray at Medjugorje, with the Queen of Peace."

The effect of the happenings of Medjugorje on both

clergy and laity alike was clear from the reaction of Bishop Kenneth Steiner of Portland Oregon, who made a private visit to Medjugorje in early November 1998.

"It is a real miracle what people experience here and take with them to their families and parish communities," he said before leaving the valley.

"Many cannot come here for various reasons, therefore they need witnesses that can help them find inner peace and discover God. And many, only when they have returned home, become aware of all that God gave them here.

"I can say the same thing about myself," he continued. "I too have become aware that I am truly blessed by coming here. I am completely renewed by coming here. I have become more aware of Christ's presence in the Sacraments, in the Church, in sacred scripture and in people in general.

"In Medjugorje, I received a new spiritual motivation.

"Perhaps some people think that we bishops and priests do not need such renewals. They would be wrong because renewal is very necessary for us.

"I have met many priests who have come to Medjugorje. They have a better idea of their priesthood. This is what I personally will take away with me."

Chapter 7

The greatest gift

What must it have been like to be a priest in Herzegovina when the first reports of apparitions of the Mother of God began to circulate? And was it because of witnessing strange or supernatural happenings that so many clergy came to believe?

A shaft of winter sunshine darts through the tall window and lights up the cool room. On the other side of the refectory table, Fr. Branimir Musa, Superior of the Franciscan Friary at Humac, some 10 kilometres from Medjugorje, leans forward in his chair and gives me a long direct look.

"I didn't see the sun spin. I didn't see the cross turn. I didn't see anything like that. But I came absolutely to the conviction that Our Lady is there, that God is present there, because nothing that people could do could bring about the fruits that have come from Medjugorje.

"I've been in the Holy Land and I've been in Lourdes, but Medjugorje has something that you can't decipher, that you can't really put into words, that you can't pin down.

"Personally, I believe that Medjugorje is a huge gift to people. The real question is, are we going to receive that gift? Are we going to respond to it?"

A tall well-built man, he wears his beliefs as openly as his brown Franciscan habit, challenging me through every step of our interview.

"People are constantly asking and worrying – what's going to happen when the apparitions cease?

"For me, that's very amusing. Why concern yourselves about that, I reply? God will worry about all that.

"For me, I don't need any signs. I don't even need the visionaries. I don't need the journalists and I don't need the commentators. I don't need anything any more. I just need to pray Medjugorje in my heart.

"Because I know that everything that's been done there, even the prayer programme, couldn't have been done without God. And when I go back to Medjugorje, I say to the Franciscans there, when I see how you live and what you are like, when I see how you do all that's done here, how you manage even to get the people confessed, then one more time I believe that Our Lady is definitely here!"

It was 1981, just two months after the apparitions began, that Branimir Musa first went to Medjugorje to see for himself what was happening there.

"I was in Bonn in Germany when I read in the newspaper that Our Lady was said to be appearing here, in this place just kilometres from where I was born. The writer said that he believed it was all nonsense and stupidity, so I decided to come here to see for myself.

"I arrived in Medjugorje just as a student, without my habit – a student who thought he knew everything – and I looked at these people and I categorised them all as fanatics. 'When the first rains fall, it will all crumble and fade away', I thought, and on I went to Italy to continue with my studies in theology."

From Italy he went to Zagreb, keeping the thought of Medjugorje well back in his mind, not even wanting to think about it.

"To be truthful", he now says, "I looked at it very much from a political point of view, taking into consideration the history of this area. In 1981, the communist ideology was beginning to be threatened and I wondered how something like a so-called apparition could threaten it further while it was becoming so unsteady."

Born in 1956 in Široki Brijeg, under that communist regime, his earliest encounters with the Franciscans were in no way spiritual.

"That's where I did my elementary school and immediately after school I would regularly creep in to steal fruit from the Franciscan orchard," he recalls with a hearty laugh.

He had one brother, Ivan, who died when he was a year old.

"My mother prayed that God would grant her another son – and I was born. But I was not very strong. During the day I would be reasonably well, but every night I became ill and sometimes even close to death. My mother made a promise to God that she would walk barefoot from Široki Brijeg to the shrine of St. Anthony in Humac if He would keep me alive.

"And I stayed alive, and when I got sense I became a priest and now I am the Superior here," he smiles, raising his hands and lifting his shoulders in that typically Croatian gesture of acceptance of the pre-ordination of it all.

His family and friends laughed, he recalls, when the strong-willed and outspoken Branimir announced his decision to join the Franciscans.

"My sister used to tease me. She used to say I'd never make it. But on 18 July 1982, I said my first Mass as an ordained priest and six days later, on 24 July, I officiated at her wedding."

There were twenty-two of them studying in his year, he recalls.

"In my naivety, I was very impressed with how many young Franciscan priests this one college would turn out, but from that number the only one who eventually became a priest was myself. For that grace, God granted 80%, the prayers of others were responsible for 15% and I myself was responsible for only 5%."

He has no doubt but that same grace led him to the gift that he considers Medjugorje.

"There I was," he observes philosophically, "believing all those who went to Medjugorje were fanatics, and extremely reserved in my opinion of the priests who would go there and confess the people. And what happened? In 1983, I was sent to a neighbouring parish and that's where my encounter with Medjugorje really began."

It was purely a working encounter at first, he recalls.

"The Franciscans in the parish of St. James in Medjugorje would call me and say, look we're mobbed – can you come in and help out with the confessions? And obviously I would agree to their request, even though I did not agree with much of what seemed to be happening there."

Yet it was through hearing the confessions of pilgrims and parishioners that Fr. Branimir Musa finally began to realise that what was happening in Medjugorje did indeed appear to be from God.

"As I sat there looking at those queues of people, sometimes I would just put my hand under my chin and observe them, and on their faces you would so often be able to see what their problems were. And I realised that while the people from my own parish, just a few kilometres away, would have come to me in confession and confessed in a very superficial way there, when they came to me in Medjugorje they would confess in a completely deep and open way.

"And simply through confessing people, I myself began to open up a bit and that ice that was within me began to melt.

"But don't get me wrong! I always revered and loved and believed in Our Lady, but now I found myself opening to Our Lady of Medjugorje and the fruits that she was beginning to bring to me and the things I was beginning to see there."

For the next three years he spent whatever time was possible in Medjugorje. And began to think how good it would be to be there more often, to pray and to confess the people and to work more on his own spiritual life.

"And that actually came about in 1995, when I was moved there and remained there until the Jubilee year of 2000. For me, this was a real learning experience and I can now say that if I hadn't come to Medjugorje I would have missed out on a great deal in my life."

His experience in the valley, he says, changed him in that he has become much more responsible in his vocation.

"I have become aware of what I am doing. I don't any longer experience any part of my priesthood as routine.

"Every word of the Bible has become more tangible, closer to me. It was in Medjugorje that I came to realise that the Gospel was not written for a time and people long ago – it's for here and it's for now.

"In the same way when you take the messages of Our Lady, many experience these like a commentary or explanation of the Bible – Our Lady telling us how we can understand this in an easier way.

"Perhaps I can explain this by saying that when a

teacher in school tells you how to behave, that carries weight. But when your mother tells you what way you're supposed to behave, that carries a completely different weight.

"And why did Our Lady appear to six children? I was a very lively child – my mother was forever explaining things to me and reprimanding me, and that's the way it is with Our Lady."

The greatest gift coming from Medjugorje, he believes, is the Sacrament of Confession.

"If it had just been one person that had confessed after twenty years, that would have been enough. Jesus said that for the sake of just one man, He would have saved the world.

"And if just one man in Medjugorje had confessed and changed his life, that would have been for me the biggest miracle, the biggest gift.

"But in my ministry there, I have seen so many receive this great gift.

"You know," he continues thoughtfully, "quite a number of priests in today's world don't like to hear confessions – they do it, but they don't necessarily like it. Yet I have heard confessions in Medjugorje for up to eight hours in one day and this experience actually relaxed me, gave me rest and peace inside.

"Through those confessions, I experienced how God is great and how man is little. But God loves man, just like that."

Despite these and other tremendous experiences during his time there, he felt no sadness in leaving the valley.

"Because my life as a Franciscan is like that. I have to go to a place and then I have to leave that place. But I know that I will always go back to Medjugorje because in that special place you will find Our Lady.

"No, she is not only there, neither is God restricted to any one place. But there, in that place, there are graces for the world. The spiritual dimension is so strong."

The afternoon has drawn on and I am due back in Medjugorje, yet it's difficult to leave the peace of this calm Franciscan friary. My own first visit to Medjugorje comes strongly to mind. I had gone there in 1985 as a Protestant journalist, I explain to this forthright priest. What I expected to find was Marian propaganda. What I actually found was the gospel message.

Fr. Branimir is amused, but not surprised.

"Let me leave you with a few thoughts," he says, as we walk through the still corridors towards the outside world.

"Have you ever thought how significant it is that when Our Lady first appeared in Medjugorje, she came with the baby Jesus in her arms? She came with one intention – to offer Jesus to us once again.

"It reminds me of a passage from that book *The Alchemist*. When the people were ordered to bow down to Our Lady, the first one said 'I'm not afraid to meet her – I'm intelligent'. The second one said 'I'm not afraid – I'm good-looking'. Another one said 'I'm worthy'. Then the fourth one comes and says, 'I'm a misery. I've made an idiot of myself all my life. When I come before her, I'm just going to juggle my balls like I did all my life in the circus'. And when he came in front of Our Lady, he did just that.

"And the story goes that little Jesus laughed and clapped his hands, and that Our Lady gave Jesus to this man so that he could cuddle Him because he had accepted Him with a humble heart.

"And that's the way it is in Medjugorje. Our Lady came with Jesus in her arms because she wanted to give Him to us all.

"All we have to do is, with love and humility, to accept Him into our lives."

"Dear Children," the Gospa said on 25 December 2000 in Medjugorje.

"Today, when God granted to me that I can be with you with little Jesus in my arms, I rejoice with you and I give thanks to God for everything He has done in this Jubilee year. I thank God especially for all the vocations of those who said 'yes' to God completely. I bless you all with my blessing and the blessing of the newborn Jesus. I pray for all of you for joy to be born in your hearts, so that in joy you too carry the joy I have today. In this Child I bring to you the Saviour of your hearts, and the One who calls you to the holiness of life. Thank you for having responded to my call."

Chapter 8

From friendship to love

Back in the living room of her family home, Vicka is busy. The following day she must leave Medjugorje to travel to Rome where, I am told by those close to her, she will meet with the Holy Father.

Her fiancé, Mario Mijatović, will travel with her. In just a few weeks from now, on 26 January, Vicka and Mario will marry in the church of St. James, Medjugorje.

It was news that came as something of a surprise to many people around the world, who had assumed that of all the visionaries Vicka was the one destined to remain unmarried and always there at her family home in Bijakovići, giving unselfishly of her time to pilgrims and priests.

None of that will change, I am assured.

Vicka will remain in the future as she is now, totally dedicated to the call of the Gospa and to the witness of the love of Jesus in our lives.

And yet, I know, many people have wondered, as they had with Marija and Ivan and the other visionaries, whether or not this was part of the Gospa's plan for the lives of the six young people who had been touched in such a heavenly way.

Watching Vicka complete the correspondence to which she must reply before leaving Bijakovići for the next week, I voice the question I'd heard asked most often over the last weeks.

Has Our Lady shown happiness for your marriage?

Vicka raises her head and the depth of her smile is answer enough.

"Yes, she has," she replies warmly.

"Always she wants our happiness, not only for this life, but for the next life too."

But has she directed you in the path that you are to take in this life, I ask?

"She never says anything special about that," Vicka replies frankly.

"She gives to us visionaries exactly what she gives to everybody else – respect for our free will. And I would never ask her anything extra about my life because I have all the privileges of seeing Our Lady every day, but also I have to take responsibility for my own life and my own decisions.

"I am sure that if I asked her, as a mother Our Lady would answer me. But I have already received so many graces and God has given each one of us free will, so how we live depends on how we receive Him in our lives."

The Virgin's concern has always been for the spiritual lives of not only the visionaries, but of all those others around the world who respond to her greeting, 'Dear Children'.

So often, Vicka reminds me, Our Lady has emphasized that she is the mother of all mankind, come to call each one of us to her son Jesus. It is how we respond to that call in our daily lives that is important.

How difficult will it be to marry somebody whose whole life is spent meeting with and ministering to so many from all over the world?

It's a question I later put to Mario, as the afternoon sun disappears from the sky and darkness approaches from the east.

"I always understood that was her mission, so I don't see it as difficult," he replies.

"I see it as absolutely wonderful and insofar as I can help Vicka with that mission I want to be there for her.

"Most of the people who come – they don't want all of her time, they just want a minute of her time. And then, when they get that minute or two and you see the joy on their faces, you say, well can I not be patient and let them have their minute?"

His love for Vicka and the joy that fills his voice when he talks about her is something special to see. Tall and good-looking, with brown waving hair, a warm smile and laughing eyes, he and Vicka share both a strong sense of humour and a depth of inner goodness that is obvious to all who meet them. Two years younger than Vicka, he is very sure that despite the pilgrims' concerns for the future, nothing will be different simply because Vicka has married.

"Vicka is not going to change," he smiles. "She will still be there, in her place, talking to the pilgrims. But perhaps the world will be a little bit happier because two people will be happy."

And he also believes that their marriage will reinforce a very strong statement for family life, as already given by the marriages of the five other visionaries of Medjugorje.

"When you see a family going into the church together, parents and children, I believe that this is sending out a message and an example to the community.

"One of the most striking things about Medjugorje is to see so many families going to Holy Mass together, every day."

Born in Sarajevo, Mario attended school there, only returning to his parents' home village of Krehin Gradac, about five kilometres from Medjugorje, during his summer holidays. After war broke out, the family returned permanently in 1992 to the safety of the region.

But his first visit back to Medjugorje in the summer of 1981, just five days after the apparitions began, is still clear in his mind.

"I came with my cousin. He was with his parents and we all went up the hill, Podbrdo. Our Lady said that we were all to kneel down and I can remember looking around and not being able to see anything supernatural, and it was a bit difficult for me to believe what was going on here. But I was curious, so I continued to climb the hill each day."

Although Mario did not know it at the time, by Sunday, 28 June 1981, that fifth day of the apparitions of the Beautiful Lady, Vicka and the five other visionaries were already beginning to experience unwanted attention from the local communist authorities.

Called in to the nearby town of Čitluk by the Secret Police the day before, they had been questioned rigorously before being taken to see a doctor, who also questioned and examined them.

Ivan was the first to be examined – a process that took over an hour – before Mirjana was called. Instead, however, Vicka entered the room and despite her age challenged the doctors to find her anything but young and healthy, before leaving and calling for a taxi to take herself and the other visionaries back to Medjugorje in the hope of meeting with the Gospa.

During the apparition that day, little Jakov asked the

Gospa (at the request of some Franciscans) what message she had for priests. The Virgin replied that they should guard the faith and believe it firmly.

By the next day, Sunday, the fifth day of the apparitions, word had spread widely across the region. A crowd estimated at some 15,000 climbed Podbrdo in the hope of experiencing something of what these six young people were seeing.

In response to Vicka's question as to what she expected of the people present, the Gospa replied that all those who did not see her should believe, just as those six who did see her.

"I didn't know either Vicka or any of the other visionaries at the time," Mario recalls.

"I knew which ones they were – their names – and I knew them to see, but I did not know them to talk to.

"As the years went on, however, I would often return to Medjugorje during my summer holidays and I came to realise what a special thing was happening there."

It wasn't until the war began, and he and his family returned to live some kilometres from Medjugorje, that Mario had the opportunity to spend much more time there.

"Then, Medjugorje became something very important for me. It became something to cling to. It was the time of my real beginning with Medjugorje because that's when I tried to start living those messages that the Gospa had been giving."

It wasn't until two years later, in 1994, that he first spoke with Vicka, he says.

"I really met her for the first time after one of her apparitions. We spoke then and I realised what a very special person she is, because immediately when you meet her you know that she's a truthful person – truthful in every way. She speaks the truth and she lives the truth that she speaks.

"Even before I became close friends with her, that was my first and strongest impression – that she was somebody who was completely sincere."

Over the coming years, he and Vicka developed a strong bond of friendship, despite the difficulties of becoming close to somebody who is constantly surrounded by people.

"Isn't it all really down to your will – if you really want something?" Mario asks.

"I really wanted to be closer to this person. I really wanted to be one of her friends. But I see now, too, in all of this, a huge act of God's providence and a huge gift for me.

"I know I can't even begin to comprehend how big an act of God's providence this is for me, but I am trying to understand it.

"You see, I believe that God gives you the people that you become close to. He puts people in your path and he gives you those special friendships that make such an impression on your life. And I see these as God's gift."

It took almost seven years before that special friendship grew into love.

"I suppose we always really understood each other and that understanding deepened all the time, until one day we realised it had turned from friendship into love," he says simply.

And if he had to describe the person who is Vicka, there is only one way, he laughs.

"Vicka is Vicka – it's enough to say that. If you want to get to know somebody, you have to go and see how they live and what they live. And what they live shows the values they have.

"Everybody who comes to Medjugorje can see the way Vicka lives and I don't need to add any more to that, except to say that I have never before met such a sincere person, somebody who is just straight across the board.

"What she says is what she does and how she lives. She has a patience that can be experienced but never described, and every emotion she feels is to be seen in her eyes."

His family, he says, could not be happier for both himself and Vicka.

"They're happy and they're excited and they're full of anticipation. My parents only have one son and for a while they were looking at me as if to say, 'It's about time you got married!' And now that the time has come, they are truly pleased."

His only sister died in a car accident at the beginning of the war, but her daughter, now aged sixteen, lives with Mario and his parents in the family home. Mario is extremely close to his niece, which is one of the reasons why, true to Croatian tradition, he and Vicka agreed to begin their married life in this house.

If he has one regret, he says, it is that Fr. Slavko could not be at their wedding. When the priest, stirred with pity for the numerous children left orphaned after the war, decided to build a Mother's Village to care for and cherish as many as possible, Mario was one of those he approached for help.

"I was on Podbrdo," he recalls quietly. "He was there too, and on our way down he called me and asked would I be interested in working on this project with him. For me, that was a huge honour and it was with all my heart that I took the job of working on the Mother's Village.

"At first, I did literally anything that needed to be done, but later I looked after the food side of things and met the pilgrims who came, to tell them about the Village. Again, I saw this as a huge gift of God's providence in my life, to be able to help all those children who had no parents, and to make them laugh."

Making them laugh again was one of Mario's greatest gifts to the children, all of whom adore him and climb all over him whenever he visits the Village.

"I feel happiest when I'm doing something that makes somebody else happy," he smiles, his whole face lit up with the same warmth and care that I have often seen on Vicka's face.

"If you're only looking after yourself in this life, then you have no hope. But if you have the privilege of always doing something for somebody else, then you can always be happy."

It was this gift, he believes, that made Fr. Slavko Barbarić such a special person.

"He gave unconditional love. His biggest virtue was that he always had time for everybody. Whether it was in the middle of the day or the middle of the night, he made time for every single person. That was the most wonderful thing about him.

"It is really only once in a century that a man like that comes along. And to have had the privilege of working alongside him is something that is impossible to describe – words are just too poor.

"In that first year of the Mother's Village, we were very close," he continues.

"To be with Fr. Slavko was a huge education. He was just an incredible example. Sometimes I would doubt his plans, what he proposed to do, and sometimes it would take me about six months to understand, 'Ah yes, he was right to do that'."

As a new chapter begins in both his and Vicka's lives, Mario has no doubt that the presence of the Gospa will play a vital role.

"Yes, I am often with Vicka during the time when Our Lady appears to her, and yes, I do feel particularly close to the Gospa during these times," he agrees.

"The apparitions are a very special experience and anybody who has the privilege of being at the apparition feels especially close to the Gospa.

"But I also believe that anybody who is living her messages could not feel far away from her and must feel her presence strongly in their lives."

If he has one message he would wish to pass on, he says, it is to emphasize the importance of the family.

"I truly believe that the family is something that's really really holy. And I have seen examples of families who are close and can stay together in love when they pray. That is the hope for my family.

"But I've also seen the opposite of that, with families who don't pray and how often they disintegrate, or if they stick together how it's only a shell.

"Yet prayer has the ability to take that shell and make it something new and whole. The Gospa has told us that."

"*Dear Children,*" the Queen of Peace said on 25 September 2000.

"*Today, I call you to open yourselves to prayer. May prayer become joy for you. Renew prayer in your families and form prayer groups. In this way, you will experience joy in prayer and togetherness. All those who pray and are members of prayer groups are open to God's will in their hearts and joyfully witness God's love. I am with you. I carry all of you in my heart and I bless you with my motherly blessing. Thank you for having responded to my call."*

Chapter 9

A life changed

Pulling aside the thick net curtain, I look out onto the hill of Podbrdo.

Set right into the hillside, the house feels part of the rocky terrain that comes close to the glass, blocking out much of the light.

Leafless bushes shake in the cold blast of the Bura, the north-east wind that blows harshly from the snow-covered mountains many kilometres away to infiltrate even the most securely closed homes in the valley.

Wrapping my woolly cardigan closer around me, I hear the voice of Vicka, who is once more talking from the steps outside the house to yet another group of pilgrims packed tightly into the yard.

Leaving the comparative shelter of the old house, I move outside to watch and to listen.

Once again, Vicka is emphasizing the importance of protecting the family in today's world. It's a concern that she has expressed frequently during our time together.

"All that this world can offer is passing by and Satan is trying to take any free moment for himself. He does that especially with the family, and wants to destroy our families.

"But this is a time of great grace," she urges, her smile reaching out to every face turned towards her.

"Our Lady tells us that.

"Are we ready to receive that grace?

"Are we ready to seek her protection?

"Are we ready to start living her messages with our hearts, so that they will change our lives and change our families and bring them closer to her son Jesus?"

Teresa (Hae Woo) Jeong reached up and snatched the piece of paper that the wind had just blown into her face. Looking down, she caught her breath.

'Programme for Medjugorje', she read, and what followed was an entire itinerary for the pilgrimage showing the date of departure, the cost, everything.

Medjugorje! She had read about it during the summer of 1996, just gone by. She didn't know exactly where it was – somewhere that was part of the geography of Europe, a long way from her home here in Seoul in South Korea. But something about the place, and the happenings that were reported there, had tugged at her heart.

She'd started to pray then, light years she felt since she had last prayed like this. One hundred and fifty mysteries she'd prayed for the opportunity to visit this place.

"Please, God!" she had begged.

"Please, Our Lady! I want to go to Medjugorje."

But it had seemed like an unreachable dream.

It still did, but now there was something else stirring inside her heart and mind.

Yesterday . . . during the parade . . . could that have been simply a coincidence or was there something more to these two strange happenings?

Yesterday, she had stood on the cold October street to watch the pilgrim statue of Fatima as it came in procession to her parish in this suburb of Seoul. As she was taking photographs of the statue and of people standing and watching it pass, she had suddenly heard a voice.

It was coming from the statue.

Or was it?

No, it was coming from inside her, but so strongly – not like a thought, more like somebody speaking inside her!

"Come closer," the voice said. "I am calling you closer to me. Come closer. Let us continue together."

As her eyes locked onto the statue of Our Lady of Fatima, Teresa had felt the words burn inside her heart. The experience had been so real. Inexplicable, but real.

Now, she looked down at the piece of paper in her hand.

Our Lady of Fatima. Our Lady of Medjugorje. Suddenly, it all made sense.

She would go to this place. How, she had no idea. She didn't have the money to travel. She didn't even have a telephone to make the call to the number on this leaflet. Her whole life, until this point, had been nothing but a series of difficulties, disappointments, terrible experiences and too many tears.

She had lived a life that was so far from the purity of this Virgin Lady that she could hardly bear to think about it. But yet, despite all that, deep inside her the conviction grew.

Somehow, she must go to Medjugorje.

This evening, sitting in the growing darkness in the house in which she stays each time she comes to Medjugorje, Teresa – shadows playing across her delicate oriental features – relives the details of a life changed. Outside, lights pick out the twin spires of the church of St. James, only metres away.

The memories are harsh, bitter, heartbreaking, joyful, significant – one emotion following another as she speaks.

From time to time she stops, lowers her head and wipes her eyes with a small white handkerchief.

She was only thirteen when her mother died. A traditional Catholic in a land of many religions, she had cherished both the spiritual and physical upbringing of her children, teaching them to love Jesus and to seek His Mother's intercession through the rosary. Every day at twelve noon, the family knelt down together to say the Angelus.

Shortly after his wife's death, Teresa's father brought another woman into his home.

"You cannot imagine what that woman was like," Teresa says softly, her gentle eyes showing a deep pain that has never completely left her.

The recollections are like something from a distorted fairy tale.

Teresa was the eldest of four children, a favourite with her mother who recognised the wealth of love and goodness in the little girl who never hesitated to help out.

"While she was alive, I was the princess of the house. When she died, everything changed and I became the gypsy."

The stories and details are too numerous and painful to go through. Over the next year, Teresa and her brothers and sister suffered every form of ill-treatment possible at the hands of their stepmother.

The deprivation of food was perhaps the hardest to bear. Given almost nothing to eat each day, the children's health suffered badly. Teresa was the worst affected, through a combination of trying to give most of what was available to her younger siblings and her stepmother's particular hatred for the child who had been so close to her mother.

The situation finally came to a head one day when Teresa returned home from school. Seeing her leave the house with nothing to eat that morning and aware that her older sister's health was deteriorating rapidly, Teresa's younger sister managed to take some food and hide it.

"I was so happy when I came home and saw the food," Teresa recalls.

"I went to take it up and eat it, and at that moment my stepmother came into the room. She saw what was happening, became very angry and beat us all. She then shouted to my father, 'I can no longer live with your children. If you want to live with me, you have to get rid of them'.

"I loved my father very much, so I said to him that if it made him happy, we would leave our home and go away and allow him to find happiness alone with this woman."

Unbelievably, her father accepted the suggestion. Within days, and just a year after their mother's death, Teresa and her brothers and sister moved into a small house on their own. From that day, at fourteen years of age, Teresa became both mother and father to the children who were then aged four, six and nine.

Because her father provided financial aid, she at first managed to continue with her schooling. Whenever possible, she spent time practising photography, which she loved and for which she had a real gift.

Then one day, without warning, the money stopped coming from their father.

"The landlord came and told us that there was no more money, so we would have to leave the house," she says softly. "I told him, untruthfully, that I had stopped my studies and started to work and that I would pay the money instead."

Her skill in photography saved them from starvation and homelessness. Finding a job with a photographic agency, she left school and became the family breadwinner. From the contacts she made in that business, she moved into another – far removed from the religious beliefs once taught her by her mother.

In a country beginning to make its presence felt on the world stage, Teresa entered the sordid world of sex tourism, using her instincts for family survival to build up a thriving agency in which she would work for thirty years. Because of her work, she says, she could not practise her faith. But somewhere, deep inside, she clung to her childhood beliefs, keeping one small cold corner of her heart for memories of the God her mother had taught her to love.

It was a life spiritually bereft, but materially successful.

"I had a standard of life that was way above other people in Korea at the time," she recalls. "Korea was quite poor then, but I had my own villa, a foreign car and my own driver. And I had married and had a family.

"But often when I was taking tourists around, I would look for a church and go in and stand at the back, and my heart would be full of sadness as I wondered why had all this happened."

More heartbreak was to follow over the coming years, when her husband left her for another, younger woman.

"I was too involved with the agency, working eighteen hours a day and caring for my children, to see what he was doing."

By now she was also pregnant for the second time. Amidst the heartbreak, she discovered that her pregnancy held dangers for both her and the baby.

"The doctors advised me to abort, but I refused. So they

told me that the only way I could get safely through this pregnancy was by lying flat in bed in hospital for five months, receiving blood transfusions."

Not once during those months did her husband come to see her. Lying in her hospital bed, Teresa spent many hours staring at a small cross hanging on the wall opposite. And through her tears, the little used prayers of her childhood slowly returned to comfort her.

During the long lonely months, Teresa struggled to renew contact with the God she had pushed out of her life. She prayed for the grace to change that life and to forgive her husband for what he was doing.

Two years before she first discovered Medjugorje, Teresa's life changed dramatically. From having everything she could require, she suddenly lost it all. The agency became bankrupt, the State revenue officials confiscated her home and anything else of value she owned and, on hearing the news, her father, with whom she had renewed contact, suffered a stroke that left him paralysed. On seeing this, his second wife left him.

Once again, Teresa was on the streets.

For the following two years, she and her family lived on the providence of others, gifts from the many she had helped financially while her agency was successful. There was enough to rent a run-down little apartment to house herself, her paralysed father and her two children.

Strangely, although they should have been starving and destitute, the family never lacked food and shelter over those two years.

Today, Teresa has no doubt but that the God who knows all that is in our hearts, and loves us with a boundless mercy and forgiveness, saw the small part of her being that all through those years continued to cry out to Him.

It was through the charity work she began to take up in the parish that she heard of the visit of the pilgrim statue of Fatima.

And found herself standing close by to where it passed.

And experienced the words, 'I am calling you closer to me . . . come closer . . . let's continue together . . . let's do it together'.

And next day caught the piece of paper floating in the air.

And renewed her prayer to go to Medjugorje.

"I had nothing – no money, no job, nothing. But I wanted so much to visit this wondrous place. And that's when the thought came into my mind – 'I'll do it. I'll restart the agency. I still have the licence. I'll bring people to Medjugorje'."

What followed was something miraculous she says now, her gentle serene face turning away from the church spires and towards me.

"I began to pray again.

"I told God that I never again wanted to do the work I'd done before. I told Him I just wanted to go to Medjugorje and I asked Him to send me the people."

But first, she had to have the facilities to run a business. And right now she had nothing.

"The following day, two people came unexpectedly to me. One was a Catholic and the other a Protestant. I had been able to help them in the past and now they just knocked on my door within hours of each other.

"One said, did you ever think of starting up your business again? And I said yes, I had, but I didn't have the money, and it would be a very different business. And when he heard, he said 'I'll rent you out a place'.

"And then a second one came later and asked had I ever thought of starting the business again, and when I told him he said, 'I'll give you a cellular phone. I'll register it in my name so the bills will come to me and I'll pay them. You just do your work'.

"Then another came the following day and said, 'I'll buy you a fax machine'.

"So suddenly, I had my licence and my premises and my telephone and a fax machine."

In June the following year, 1997, in time for the sixteenth anniversary of the beginning of the apparitions, Teresa brought her first group of thirty pilgrims to Medjugorje. Every month since then, she has brought a new group.

The wealth she had acquired with her previous agency has never been repeated, neither does Teresa wish for it. She still lives in that poor little apartment and any profit she makes is spent bringing those who can't afford it to this place of peace and prayer. But she has returned, tenfold, to the practice of the Catholic faith her mother taught her.

Teresa has also experienced another miracle in her life.

As the peace and love of Jesus and the Gospa filled her life and home and family, her husband's thriving factory businesses crashed on the stock market. While financial ruin faced him, the woman he now lived with became increasingly discontented.

Beginning to visit his family again, he noticed how, despite the poverty of her surroundings, Teresa was full of inner peace. And wondered what had brought this about.

In September 1997, Teresa experienced a sense of tremendous healing during a visit to Medjugorje. Remembering an old Korean custom, she wrote the names of both her husband and the woman with whom he lived on a piece of paper and placed this on the altar in the church of St. James. Offering the Mass for them, she knew that the God of love and forgiveness had touched her with His healing power.

Returning home, she found her husband sitting there.

What she didn't know was that he had come to say goodbye to his children, before emigrating. Brought up as a Jehovah's Witness, he had occasionally, against his will, accompanied Teresa to Mass during the early days of their marriage. Now, as he sat here in this tiny room, he felt an overwhelming urge to go once again to a Catholic church.

Finding one a short time later, he entered, sat down and almost immediately experienced a tremendous sense of peace. It was the same peace he had sensed in Teresa's apartment, he realised, despite the poverty and humility of its surroundings.

His journey since then has been long, often difficult and even turbulent. But this evening, as Teresa recalls the events that led her towards a new life, he joins us in the darkened room.

It is his second visit to Medjugorje.

The first time, he spent every day drinking in one of the restaurants. But gradually, a change came about. This time, she smiles, he's the first to enter the church each morning, where he kneels right in front of the altar. He's taking instruction in the Roman Catholic faith and is back living with his family.

It's he who now looks after Teresa's father, as the old man's health deteriorates. He changes his nappies, cooks his meals, baths him and prays with him.

Looking back, Teresa can see with great clarity the road that led her from darkness to a changed life.

"I can still feel my mother's finger touching me here, on my heart, and saying 'Here! That's where your conscience is – and that's where the Lord is'.

"And after she died and our lives became so difficult, I would write in my diary for comfort every night and for some reason I always addressed what I wrote to God.

"At the top of each page, I would draw a little cross and say 'Praised be the Lord', as my mother had taught me, and then I would begin to write. 'Dear God', I would begin – and it's only now that I realise that this was a prayer and that God heard the prayer of a child's heart.

"And sometimes, when I look about me in this special place of Medjugorje, I wonder – why is Our Lady sending me all this love in my life because for so many years I never gave her any love?

"But it's then I remember how, as a child, I used to pray the rosary on my knees beside my mother. And even though my knees would be hurting and I would be shifting from side to side and sometimes I became impatient, I now realise how every little prayer, even those from a small child, means so much to Our Mother who repays it in abundance."

"*Dear Children*," the Gospa said on 25 June 1997, just days after Teresa arrived in Medjugorje for the very first time.

"*Today, I am with you in a special way and I bring you my motherly blessing of peace. I pray for you and I intercede for you before God, so that you may comprehend that each of you is a carrier of peace. You cannot have peace if your heart is not at peace with God. That is why, little children, pray, pray, pray, because prayer is the foundation of your peace. Open your heart and give time to God so that He will be your friend. When true friendship with God is realised, no storm can destroy it. Thank you for having responded to my call.*"

Chapter 10

Prayer and fasting

An oasis of peace in the midst of war – this was how many described Medjugorje during those horror-filled years that ravaged the Balkans and changed the face of the former Yugoslavia forever.

Over two million displaced from their homes and the lands of their ancestors to end up homeless and poverty-stricken in refugee camps or broken-down buildings. Thousands of women raped. Untold thousands of men, from boys to grandfathers, butchered, then buried in mass graves. And thousands of children orphaned or separated hopelessly from their parents and families.

Many of the survivors made their way to Medjugorje, to this place of peace in a world gone mad. It was protected, they heard, by the Virgin's mantle.

All round it, bombs rained down on villages and lives were lost. Just 30 kilometres away, the ancient town of Mostar crumbled beneath the onslaught of destruction, the pounding of the guns heard in the valley of the Virgin.

But Medjugorje remained untouched.

Two bombs had been dropped, they said. One landed on the outskirts of the village, destroying only a cowshed. The other failed to explode.

A European newspaper carried the story of pilots sent to bomb the region, with particular emphasis on the valley that had become for many a Marian shrine. They lost their way, the pilots told reporters. When they reached the airspace close to the valley, a thick cloud blocked their vision. Despite attempting to fly through it and even around it, they could see nothing. So they left the area, jettisoning their bombs over waste ground.

And then began the human trail of misery as, in battered cars and broken-down lorries, on foot and carrying tales of horror, refugees flooded into the valley.

The children were the most pitiful – faces like masks, hiding the unspeakable things they'd seen and experienced.

And while international aid poured in from agencies, founded so often by those whose own hearts had been touched by the Queen of Peace, others asked – could it all have been avoided? Or was that a question too naive even to be contemplated?

From the very beginning, the Gospa had asked for prayer and fasting. Only in this way, she said, could we find peace – a peace that began in the heart and spread to the family, to those around us, and from there to the whole world.

On the third day of the apparitions, she had appeared to Marija carrying a large cross.

"*Peace, Peace, Peace and only Peace,*" she had said, her expression unbearably sad and what seemed like tears in her voice. "*Peace must reign among God and man, and also among men.*"

On numerous occasions over the following years, she repeated her call to peace.

"*Dear Children,*" she had said on 6 September 1984. "*Without prayer there is no peace. Therefore I say to you, dear children, pray at the foot of the cross for peace. Thank you for having responded to my call.*"

On 14 August of that same year, the vigil of the Feast of the Assumption, and during an unexpected apparition to

Ivan as he prepared to go to the church for evening Mass, she had given the following message and asked that it be related to the people:

"I would like the people to pray along with me these days. And to pray as much as possible. And to fast strictly on Wednesdays and Fridays, and every day to pray at least one rosary – the joyful, sorrowful and glorious mysteries."

The Gospa had asked that we accept this message with a firm will, Ivan added.

On 25 April 1992, as war continued to rage through the former Yugoslavia, she gave the following message:

"Dear Children. Today also I invite you to prayer. Only by prayer and fasting can war be stopped. Therefore, my dear little children, pray and by your life give witness that you are mine and that you belong to me, because Satan wishes in these turbulent days to seduce as many souls as possible. Therefore, I invite you to decide for God and He will protect you and show you what you should do and which path to take. I invite all those who have said 'yes' to me to renew their consecration to my Son Jesus and to His Heart and to me, so that we can take you more intensely as instruments of peace in this unpeaceful world. Medjugorje is a sign to all of you and a call to pray and live the days of grace that God is giving you. Therefore, dear children, accept the call to prayer with seriousness. I am with you and your suffering is also mine. Thank you for having responded to my call."

Even wars could be stopped by prayer and fasting.

If we believed it possible, what miracles could have been achieved in the lives of so many, in countries all over the world?

Over twenty million people had visited Medjugorje over the last twenty years. How many of us had truly responded to her call?

In the silence of the room, I realise that Vicka has finished her writing and is waiting for me to continue our conversation. But some words she had spoken earlier have returned to haunt me.

"She is sad," Vicka had told me.

"She says, 'I have so many messages to give you, but I cannot give them to you because the messages I have already given are not received'.

"She says, 'I would be most happy if you received the messages with your heart and every day lived them, going step by step forward'."

And again, the inadequacy of our response – my own response – triggers a deep sadness in my heart.

In my mind I see the faces of the orphans in the Mother's Village, the hopelessness of so many who have lost everything and for whom life is an unbearable daily struggle. The families and the old people who wish only for a place, once more, to call their own.

Some of this I share briefly with Vicka.

"Yes, she wants us to be carriers of her peace and to pray for peace in the world," she responds. "Firstly in our own hearts, then in our families, in our communities and after that to pray for peace throughout the world.

"But Our Lady says that if we are praying for peace in the world and we don't have peace in our own hearts, then that prayer is not as strong.

"So it must all begin with us, in our hearts."

And the Gospa has already advised us how to do this, Vicka adds.

"She has told us to take strength from the words of God in the Holy Bible. To read a few lines every day and to have the Holy Bible in a central place in our homes."

From there, Vicka continues, we can begin gradually to grow in love and peace, using the tools the Gospa has recommended – prayer and fasting.

"Yes," she smiles, as if reading my mind, "I know it is difficult. So many people come for example and say, 'Vicka, I find it so hard to fast', but I remind them of what Our Lady says – 'If you fast out of love for me and Jesus, everything will be possible'. The only thing that is missing is our strong will.

"And Our Lady is a real mother, who understands how weak we are. She understands all this. She speaks of those who are sick, for example. She doesn't ask for them to fast on bread and water. She suggests, instead, that they give up something that they like a lot.

"But for those who are healthy and who say that they cannot fast, that they have a headache or they feel dizzy, she says again, 'If you fast out of love for me and Jesus, everything will be possible'.

"Prayer and fasting are our most powerful weapons and so often Our Lady has told us that with these and with other sacrifices, however small, we can change not only our own lives, but the lives of people around us.

"And yes, that with prayer and fasting, we can stop even wars."

Chapter 11

From war to peace

Zvonko Čoja looks out the window into the darkness of the night. Somewhere, up on the mountain of Križevac, lights glimmer faintly as pilgrims brave the cold and harshness of the wind to make their pilgrimage of prayer to the foot of the great cross. There, in the early years of the apparitions, the Gospa said she prayed often to her Son for the conversion of sinners.

The darkness outside is nothing to the darkness that fills Zvonko's mind as haltingly, and stopping often to wipe his eyes, he recalls the horror of those years that ravaged his country and took from him all that he once owned.

In this valley of peace, he relives the effects of a war that left his family homeless and destitute. And the renewal and healing that has strangely come from it all.

It had all been so normal before war broke out, he begins.

"We had everything we needed. I worked and so did Ljubica, my wife, and our three children were happy. We lived in a beautiful place, about four and a half kilometres from the town of Konjic. Even Austria couldn't hold a candle to that place up there, with its forests and mountains and rivers.

"My son, Bojan, was an altar boy in the church, but later," he hesitates, pain filling his eyes, "afterwards, like all the other children I know, after the war he was like somebody ten years older because of what he had experienced."

Like most of the men in his region, Zvonko Čoja did not wait to be conscripted when war broke out and the weight first of Serbia and then of the Muslim forces invaded the area.

"How could I not go to war when all my people were going? How could I let others defend me and my family?"

His family, like all those around them, were moved first to a place of greater safety and then, as war raged across the area, taken from one town to another in cars, lorries or freezer trucks, whatever was available, until eventually they reached the safety of Medjugorje.

All they took with them were the clothes they could carry in their arms.

"Why Medjugorje? Because this is where the people open-heartedly welcomed them," he says simply.

As he watched the truck leaving with his family, he felt an enormous sense of sadness and loss.

"I didn't know if I would ever see them again."

No words could describe the misery of that war, he says.

"Ninety per cent of the people who were in that war with me had never before held a gun in their hands. They didn't know how to hold one. They didn't know how to take aim. But what choice did we have? We had to defend our homes."

He was sent to defend the front line, some distance away from his own home. There, he says, he witnessed things that nobody should have to see. Time and again since then, he has tried to banish those scenes from his mind. But they refuse to go.

For years afterwards he admits, he could not sleep at

night, the darkness bringing with it the living nightmares he had witnessed.

One of these has refused to relinquish any of its horror over time.

"It was a little girl," he says, a tortured look coming into his eyes. "She was only about seven years of age, the same age as my daughter Daniella.

"They were trying to escape across a bridge – she and her family. The father stepped on a mine and it exploded, taking with it half of his foot. The mother died instantly. And the little girl . . ." Breaking down, he stops to wipe away the tears from his face. "The little girl, one of her legs was blown off from the knee and the other from the thigh. The bones were gone and all that was left hanging was skin.

"I was on a hill about 70 metres away when it happened. I saw the explosion and I heard the screams and I ran down from the hill right onto the bridge, without even thinking of any danger because at a time like that you just react.

"I picked up the little girl to carry her to a safer place and all I remember is her screaming and crying out, 'Don't leave my mammy there on the bridge, don't leave my mammy'. But her mammy was dead – and half an hour later she died, too."

The horror of the scene will never leave him, he says.

"It's because of things like this that I couldn't sleep at night.

"They laid them out – the mother and the little girl – in the chapel that night and it was heartbreaking to see them lying there together.

"And every time I tried to sleep after that, my mind went back to what I saw."

It was after another horrifying incident that he and

other men in the area realised they could no longer ensure the safety of their families and so they rushed them away.

"My wife's brother and three of his friends were with us on the front line. One night, they decided to go back to their village, to see if it was safe. They went straight into the hands of the enemy. Some of our other neighbours saw it all, but could do nothing.

"One of them tried to get away. He was machine-gunned in the back as he ran. They got my wife's brother and his friends. They cut them to pieces while they were still alive. With my own ears, I could hear my brother-in-law screaming for help, but none of us could help him. We could not even make it across the land, with the force of men that were there."

Stopping to hold his face in his hands and stem the flow of tears, he continues.

"They put needles through their eyes. They cut off their ears, their noses. When they left and we went to recover the bodies next morning, I found my brother-in-law with his genitals stuffed into his mouth."

For a whole year after that, he never saw his family. Every day of that year, he says, was filled with horror. As the war raged, firstly against one enemy and then another, Zvonko Čoja found himself in the strange position of helping both Serbian and Muslim civilians. In a conflict which knew no bounds, and which brought out the savagery in most, the goodness and humanity that is part of his own being kept him from descending into barbarism.

"War brings terrible atrocities," he says.

"There were times when I could have raped and times when I could have robbed someone of what I wanted. There were times when I could have crushed a man in the palm of my hand and done whatever I wanted to do. But

I never did these things.

"How could I rape? I have a wife and two daughters. My mother taught me always to put myself in the shoes of others.

"I could have made huge amounts of money robbing, thieving, selling women – but I didn't do any of these things.

"I lost everything – but God gave much back to me in another way, an honest way.

"I can look a Serb in the eye. I can look a Muslim in the eye. I have kept my dignity."

Religion never played much part in his life before this, he admits.

"I was never a church-goer. For fifteen years, I never confessed. So, for fifteen years I never received Communion.

"And then one day, after I came to Medjugorje, a friend, Ante Mužić, who has done so much for me since I came here, brought me to Široki Brijeg, to a Franciscan I had much admiration for – Fr. Svetozar, who is worth his weight in gold.

"I saw that during the war. Four or five times, he went through the enemy lines – through the Serbian lines, through the Muslim lines, putting his life on the line to confess the people, to say Mass, to bring humanitarian aid.

"I confessed to Fr. Svet – for the first time in fifteen years – and after those terrible things that had happened, I gained a peace. Not just any type of peace, but a really good peace. And I started to go back to Mass."

Before that, while the war still raged, he managed to get back to his home, just once. It was the last time he was to do so.

"I cried like a child. It was so hard for me to be there, alone. On the one hand, I was glad that Lubjica and my children were gone, that they were safe. But on the other it was so heartbreaking.

"Earlier, just after they left and before things became impossible in the area, I would occasionally return to our home. There, I looked at this little image of St. Anthony of Padua holding the child Jesus and many times I pleaded, 'Oh, St. Anthony – please either take me or get me out of here and reunite me with my family'.

"And eventually, my St. Anthony introduced me to another Anthony in Medjugorje and I know Our Lady sent me to him. Now, when I look back, I see that Our Lady was saying to my wife – 'Go to Medjugorje. In Medjugorje everything will work out'."

It wasn't until a truce was brokered between the Croats and Muslims, and a United Nations convoy arrived in the area, that it became possible for Zvonko to go in search of his family.

"The UN came in their trucks and brought us over the occupied territories, to safety. I remember lying back in the lorry, after a year of conflict, and saying, 'Thank you, God. Thank you, Jesus'.

"We got to Ljubuški, about eight kilometres from Medjugorje, and there was a welcome committee there to greet us. But I didn't want the meal that was waiting for us and I didn't want the party. I only dreamed of meeting my wife and children again. At times, I had thought that we would never see each other again.

"So I came on to Medjugorje. I didn't even know what house they were in – just that they were safely here."

All during that year, Ljubica, with her son Bojan and daughters Ivana and Daniella, had prayed for his safe return. So many never returned.

That day started in sadness like any other, Ljubica now

recalls, and ended in total happiness.

A man in the village of Medjugorje had offered shelter to the family, a room where they could sleep and a place to shower and eat. They had been there for a year.

She had just gone up the outside stairs, to change the bedclothes, when she heard a voice calling in the courtyard below.

"Where's Ljubica Čoja? Can anybody tell me where she is?"

Ljubica called back. "Who's looking for me?"

She couldn't believe that it might be her husband, she says.

"It felt like it was the very same second I heard her voice that I ran into the house," Zvonko recalls.

"I threw my arms around Ljubica and then walked into the room. My youngest daughter Daniella was sitting on the couch. When she saw me, she jumped right from the couch, on top of the table, and across to me.

"For three days, I didn't let her out of my arms. Even when I went into the bathroom, she would sit outside the door and say, 'I'm afraid that you're going to go away again'."

That was seven years ago. But for most of those years, life has been hard and fraught with anxiety, as Zvonko Čoja and his family lived in poverty, as did so many other refugees. Their home was a broken-down two-roomed ruin, with no running water. Every night, they were kept awake by the scuttling of mice across the floor and under the makeshift beds. They had no bathroom and their toilet was a bucket in the corner of an adjoining roofless outhouse.

But the Gospa who had brought them to Medjugorje had not left them to fend alone. Their plight touched the heart of a pilgrim, who returned home to raise money to build them a little bungalow. And Zvonko found work, cleaning around the church, gardening, caretaking – anything that would help him provide for his family.

Most importantly, the peace of Medjugorje began slowly and gently to sink into their hearts and to heal the wounds inflicted by war and loss.

Ljubica found both peace and physical healing of several ailments when Fr. James, a very special priest from India, came to the parish to give a healing retreat.

And Zvonko found his initial reservations about the authenticity of the apparitions at Medjugorje challenged in a very real way.

"No, I didn't believe immediately," he says frankly.

"I found it difficult to accept so readily that such a thing could be happening – that the Mother of God could be coming here, to this place, in my country. But over the time that I have been here, I have had several experiences that have made me believe. Experiences that cannot be simply explained away."

The one that finally removed his remaining reservations happened in July 2001.

"I had a bad wound on my hand," he says. "If I clenched my fist, which I did all the time I was working, the cut would immediately burst open again and bleed. I had tried everything possible to heal that wound. I used every kind of cream or ointment that was possible to use, but still it remained and grew worse every day.

"Then here, in the middle of summer last year, in the middle of the drought when there hadn't been a drop of rain for months and everything was completely dried out –

even the grass had turned yellow – and the temperatures were higher than they had been for over thirty years, and there was no hope of rain for at least a month, something incredible happened.

"From the side of the knee – just a little bit lower than the knee – on the statue of the Risen Jesus, down behind the church here in Medjugorje, these drops of liquid started to appear, like tears falling down. It went on for almost two weeks and everybody around came to see it and to rub pieces of cloth in it and to place this liquid on themselves.

"And several times, I went down to that statue and I took a drop of that liquid on my finger and made the sign of the cross on the wound that wouldn't heal and massaged the liquid into it."

By the second day, he says, the wound had started to heal. Soon it had completely disappeared, never to return.

"It's as if God was saying to me, 'Will you just believe a little bit more?'

"And I did. How could I not? And now, when I go to pray, it is different. Because it's not just with the lips, but humbly, with the heart. And at those times, everything else leaves me – all the problems, the bad memories, everything."

"Dear Children," the Gospa said on 25 May 2001.

"At this time of grace, I call you to prayer. Little children, you work much but without God's blessing. Bless and seek the wisdom of the Holy Spirit to lead you at this time, so that you may comprehend and live in the grace of this time. Convert, little children, and kneel in the silence of your hearts. Put God in the centre of your being so that, in that way, you can witness in joy the beauty that God continually gives in your life. Thank you for having responded to my call."

Chapter 12

Death into life

"Dear Children," the Gospa said on 25 December 1996.

"Today, I am with you in a special way, holding little Jesus in my lap, and I invite you, little children, to open yourselves to His call. Little children, joyfully live the messages of the Gospel, which I am repeating in the time since I am with you. Little children, I am your Mother and I desire to reveal to you the God of love and the God of peace. I do not desire for your life to be in sadness, but that it be realised in joy for eternity, according to the Gospel. Only in this way will your life have meaning. Thank you for having responded to my call."

'I do not desire for your life to be in sadness, but that it be realised in joy for eternity . . .'

Outside, the skies grow dark and rain begins to fall, not gently but in a huge deluge of water that beats down on the village of Bijakovići, hammering against the roofs and cascading down into the narrow roads. Locals and pilgrims alike rush for cover, leaving the village as if deserted.

As the rain and wind continue to rage and the heavy clouds overhead block out the mid-morning light, taking away whatever little warmth there was and completely obliterating the cross on top of Križevac, I am reminded of how fleeting are the things of this world and how dark our lives without the hope of the world to come.

"So many people fear death," I observe slowly to Vicka.

"What would you say to these and to all those who mourn?"

A swift smile at the blackness of my thoughts and a slight shake of her head before she answers.

"We are just passing through here – that is what Our Lady says. Because life goes on.

"If you believe in eternal life, then you just pass by, you just keep on living. There is just a passing between this world and the next."

But we should prepare for that passing, I suggest?

"Yes of course, but we have to remove the fear that holds us back, because fear never comes from God.

"And in our preparation, there should be nothing special like, for instance, deciding to kneel down and pray, 'Please God, let me go to heaven'.

"Our preparation should just be in living a normal Christian life and praying to God and keeping close to Him every day. Because if He is in the centre of our lives, then what do we have to fear? If we try to live our lives close to Him, there can be no fear of the future or of death.

"Nor do we need to fear for those we know who have died, but who tried to live their lives as best they can and with love for God in their hearts. We should think of them only with happiness."

The rain gathers even more in ferocity, beating against the windows and hopping noisily off the balcony outside, making conversation impossible for a couple of minutes.

Waiting for it to pass, my mind focuses on what Vicka has been saying.

'. . . think of them only with happiness'.

Not just empty words on her part, I realise, as I recall

how I'd been told about the sudden death of her brother-in-law, Nedjo – husband of her older sister, Mica.

Many of those who saw her around this time remarked on how she was far more joyful than saddened by his death, although obviously missing his presence greatly and concerned for the shock of her sister.

And shock it had been.

Nedjo had always been close to Vicka, very much part of the family and always a tremendously strong support to the visionary. Full of life and laughter and good humour and great love for the Gospa and her Son, he had been part of the prayer group that grew up around the visionaries during those earlier years, praying and playing his guitar and singing with so much love and conviction.

It was fitting, so many said, that when he died, it was just after being with Ivan and the prayer group, during an apparition.

Ivan had come up to him afterwards, saying "I don't know why, Nedjo, but all through the apparition Our Lady kept looking over and smiling at you".

Nedjo had been touched by the revelation, saying to those around him 'How wonderful it must be to see Our Lady smile. I wonder when I will leave this world and see that for myself'.

Leaving the group, he returned to his car with his wife and teenage son. Just after getting in, he slumped over the wheel.

"Stop that messing, Nedjo," his wife said, adding as he didn't reply – "Nedjo, stop that, you are beginning to frighten me."

His son, sitting in the back of the car, realised that something was dreadfully wrong. Jumping out, he dashed around to the driver's door and pulled it open. As he did,

Nedjo fell sideways into his arms. His son only had time to cry out how much he loved his father before Nedjo passed from this world to the place where at last he could see the loving smiles of the Gospa and her Son.

"I don't see any great sadness in death," Vicka says as I mention Nedjo.

"I know that Nedjo is happy. And as much as God gives us the gift of life, He gives us the gift of death. There is no difference.

"Many parents say, for example, when they lose their children – 'Why, God, did you take them?' They are sad when God takes, but they are joyful when God gives, and they don't see that it is the same when He gives as when He takes. Each is a gift.

"Because Our Lady says that we have to be happy both when He gives and when He takes.

"If we only knew what happiness awaits us in heaven, we could never be sad.

"So how wonderful it would be if we could just say thank you to God when He gives us those we love and tell Him that because we have faith in His promises, we also allow Him to take them back, knowing they are going into such joy."

Chapter 13

Melting the sorrow

"I do not desire for your life to be in sadness, but that it be realised in joy for eternity, according to the Gospel. Only in this way will your life have meaning."

The words of the Gospa's message on 25 December 1996 echoed in Lynn Hoffman's aching heart as she sat in her bedroom in the house of visionary Mirjana Dragicević Soldo. It was 2 January 1997, her birthday, and only weeks after the death of her beloved husband, just before Thanksgiving the previous November.

They should have been here together, for the very first time. Although Lynn had been travelling regularly to Medjugorje since September 1990, her husband had never come with her. Suffering from claustrophobia, he had felt unable to contemplate the long journey from his home in California to this valley in Eastern Europe.

It was Mirjana who had finally persuaded him to travel with Lynn. She had written to him, a beautiful letter asking him to come to Medjugorje for his and Lynn's 40th wedding anniversary. And to Lynn's surprise, he had agreed.

Six weeks before travelling, he had died very suddenly, leaving Lynn heartbroken. Afterwards, she felt there was now no reason to travel to Medjugorje on the date arranged.

"Then Mirjana called me," she says simply, as we sit in front of a big log fire while outside the light fades from the sky and the hills surrounding Medjugorje disappear into the darkness.

"She told me that despite my sorrow, I must still come to Medjugorje. And I asked why? The trip had been to celebrate our anniversary – and now there seemed no reason to make it. But she said, 'You must' and so I talked with my spiritual advisor, Fr. Bob, and he said, 'Well, if Mirjana says you must, then you must'. And so I came."

Her sorrow was so deep all the way over the Atlantic that she could scarcely bear it.

The peace of Medjugorje brought some relief, but still the ache remained.

As she sat alone in her bedroom, her birthday meaning little to her, Mirjana knocked on the door and entered the room.

"It was the day of Mirjana's special apparition. The daily apparitions had ceased after she received the tenth secret, but for some time Our Lady had been appearing to her privately on the second day of every month. When she came into my room, she told me that she would be having the apparition there with me.

"It was such a wonderful experience and gave me so much peace and consolation. And during the apparition, Mirjana told me, she recommended me to Our Lady, saying that my heart was sad because I should have been there with my husband.

"Then she told me what Our Lady's reply had been – 'She's mine. I need her'.

"At that apparition, in fact, Our Lady also told Mirjana that she would continue to appear to her on the second day of every month, but that the time had now come for these special visits to be shared with everyone. So, from that date on, 2 January 1997, Mirjana's monthly apparitions are always held in public, often in Cenacalo, and with many people present."

The Gospa's words for Lynn were like a balm of consolation being placed on the heavy burden of sorrow in her heart.

In the days that followed, at Mirjana's suggestion, she spent many hours in the Church of St. James, praying and trying to discern just why and how the Gospa could possibly need her.

"Pray and you'll know," the visionary had smiled when she asked for advice, so Lynn did just that.

"I prayed and I prayed and when it was time for me to leave Medjugorje I turned to Mirjana and said, 'Well, all I can think is that She wants me to bring pilgrims to Medjugorje'. And Mirjana said, 'Well, that's what I think, too'.

"And after that, it all just happened and that's how I know that it truly was from God. Because six months later, I brought my first group of pilgrims with me and now, this is my fifty-fourth visit to the valley."

The memory of that very first visit, however, in September 1990, is still fresh in Lynn's mind. As is the compelling urge that led her to make the pilgrimage.

She had first heard of the apparitions of the Virgin in Medjugorje from a friend.

"I had never heard of either the apparitions or the place, but when she explained to me all that was happening there, I knew instantly that it was real. And it just touched my heart to the point that I couldn't even understand what was happening inside me. But right from that first knowledge, it became such a profound part of my life.

"We started a Medjugorje prayer group and we held an information centre at our church every Sunday. We showed videos of Medjugorje – and still I hadn't been. But yet, I believed."

She hadn't been born into the Catholic faith. "I was raised nothing – I had no spirituality, but when I met my husband he was a Catholic and he was such a good example. And about twenty years before ever setting foot in Medjugorje, I was received into the Catholic faith.

"I always did the right thing, as far as not missing Mass and that was concerned, and I loved the church. But the deep love wasn't there. That came after my first visit to Medjugorje."

She smiles when she recalls her husband's reaction when she returned home from pilgrimage. "I had been so touched by my experience of Medjugorje that, as I left the valley, I cried for almost an hour because I was so sure that I would never return there. You see, we weren't the sort of couple that ever went anywhere without each other, so this trip had been something very different.

"And when I eventually arrived home, my husband saw that something had touched me deeply. He was cautious in his response for some time – in fact, about six months after I got home, he said to me one day, 'Don't become a fanatic'. I asked, 'What are you talking about?' And he said, 'You're different – you've changed so much'. And I really truly didn't know what he meant.

"So then I started thinking and I realised that I was not the same person. 'Fanatic' was not a good word to describe me, but I guess he feared the change he saw in me.

"It was just that my love for Our Lord after being here was so profound that everything was different. I no longer was interested in anything material. My only life, since then, is for my Lord."

Had her faith been so much different in the twenty

years she spent in the Catholic Church before visiting Medjugorje?

"Yes, it was different," she replies softly.

"I loved being a Catholic and was very grateful for the faith I had found. But as I said, the deep love wasn't there. Now, when I think about going to Mass and receiving Jesus, my heart just jumps for joy – every day. Not to receive Communion is just not possible for me. And when I look at Jesus in the Eucharist, in the Blessed Sacrament during our holy hours in the church here in Medjugorje, it just moves me in a way that is almost impossible to describe."

Her desire to visit Medjugorje that first time was something else she finds difficult to describe.

"I just believe that I was called," she says with a quiet certainty. "I had such a strong calling in my heart, I didn't understand it. I didn't know why I had to go. Then the war started in Croatia and afterwards in Bosnia, and still I had this strong calling in my heart. I just knew I had to come over.

"My husband was very much against it because of the war and not knowing what way it would go. He would say, 'Why? Why would you have to go?' And all I could reply was, 'I don't know. I only know I have to go'.

"Then every group I signed up with was cancelled because of the war, but finally I found one that was prepared to travel.

"And when I arrived in Medjugorje, I knew how right it was to be there. I was so emotional and just overwhelmed with the sense of being in this special place where Our Lady came, every day, to bring us closer to Jesus."

Despite her fears that it might be her only trip and her deep reluctance to travel without her husband, Lynn found herself being called back to Medjugorje many times over the following years.

"It all just happened. When I returned, I just couldn't stop talking about the peace and spirituality of this special place and people began to say, 'Well, I'd like to go, but only if you come with me'. And it just went from there. My husband gave me his blessing to go – and I went."

Right through the war years, Lynn Hoffman continued to visit Medjugorje, responding not only to her own spiritual call, but to the urgent need of those she saw.

"We began to bring medical supplies and humanitarian aid, and the doctors from Mostar hospital – in a region where there was bitter fighting – would send an ambulance to pick up the supplies. We learned to bring everything in really old battered suitcases that we picked up from thrift stores, so that they didn't look like they contained anything worth stealing. We'd tape them up and sometimes they contained $10,000-worth of antibiotics and other medicines.

"At other times, they told us that it was blood they desperately needed and when I explained this to the pilgrims they always responded so generously and gave blood.

"And yes, it was dangerous at times and I was shot at on more than one occasion, but at no time did I feel that I should not be doing this."

There were times, however, when others questioned the sense of what she was doing.

"We would hold Medjugorje meetings and people would come up to my husband and practically attack him. They'd say things like, 'How can you let your wife go out there to that war-torn country and do work like that? She could be killed'.

"And I remember this one time I heard him reply – and I was so proud of him. He just said, 'Well, last week there were two people killed in Stockville, about twenty miles away from here, but nobody's ever been killed in Medjugorje'. And it was such a great answer."

Several things made a deep impression on Lynn's mind and heart during those early visits.

"The queues for confession all round the church; climbing Podbrdo and Križevac in such a prayerful atmosphere; how crowded the church always was, with people trying to almost push their way in, whereas at home they would have been trying to push their way out! Yes, it was all so holy that your heart could not fail to be touched.

"And then there were other things. For instance, during the war we would have to take a list of our pilgrims (which had already been provided to our Embassy) down to the police station, so that if ever we were attacked they would know who was travelling. And when I would go into the police station, there were crucifixes on the wall and rosary beads hanging, and the same at the post office – crucifixes on the walls and pictures of the Blessed Mother. I had never seen anything like that anywhere else before. I was just so touched by the devotion to Our Lady.

"And then, to walk by Colombo's restaurant, close to the church, and see groups of people sitting there and praying the rosary in front of everyone walking by! It was just so wonderful.

"Then there were the visionaries – to see them and to talk to them and to know that they had been chosen by God for a very special mission, and coming to realise that they are so human, just like the rest of us. I had expected them to be different, but they are so normal, even though they are obviously extremely holy and have been chosen so specially."

Returning home from Medjugorje that January 1997, just days after what should have been her 40th wedding anniversary, and with the knowledge of the Gospa's words 'She's mine. I need her' burning in her heart, Lynn gave the whole idea of organising pilgrimages some very deep thought.

"I still had a lot of numbness inside because of my husband's death. He hadn't been sick – he just had a heart attack and died so suddenly. It was such a shock and I missed him so greatly. I had never lived alone, never, so I was trying to get used to so many changes in my life.

"But through it all, I felt Our Lady's presence in my life, and that and receiving Jesus in the Eucharist every day gave me strength and eventually a deep peace."

Inside, too, grew the conviction that to take as many people as possible to experience the deep peace and healing of Medjugorje was what she was being asked to do.

"And when I look back, I can see that all along I was being groomed for what I'm doing now, because certainly Our Lord knew that he was taking my husband to be with Him and He knew that I would need something to do and that if it was for Him I would have the heart to do it."

Where to begin was not an easy task.

"I didn't know anything about the travel business. I had never travelled anywhere except to Medjugorje. I didn't have any sense of gathering people together. I had no mailing list – nothing. But somehow it all just happened and God put in my path the people to help me and through word of mouth it all began to grow.

"At first, I thought I would come twice a year and then I just had to start scheduling more often so that the groups wouldn't be too big, because it's hard to cope with a very big group."

She chuckles when she recalls that very first group, some six months or so later.

"It was so difficult. I ended up with 50 people and the travelling was awful. We had to come through Rome and stay overnight on the way in two different hotels and deal with two different coach companies. I was new to it all and I really didn't have the slightest idea of what to do. All I wanted was to take people to Our Lady, but I didn't want all this other stuff.

"So the next time I set about organising a pilgrimage I said, 'Blessed Mother, I will take pilgrims as often as you want me to, as many as you want, but please – don't ever give me 50 again!'

"And the next time I got 51, so I said 'Ah, I get the picture. It's not what I want!' Since then, I've never put a limit on it and we come twice a month and at times the group has numbered 75."

Apart from the practical arrangements concerning travel from the United States to Eastern Europe, Lynn had no idea where or how she was going to house her pilgrims. The answer came when she collected Mirjana and her husband, Marko, from the airport to attend a Marian conference near Lynn's home, about 60 miles east of San Francisco.

"I had first met Mirjana in 1990, during that very first visit I made to Medjugorje. Although she was pregnant with her oldest child, Marija, she walked across the field from her new home to talk to our group. I remember thinking her house was quite large, but it was only when we were talking in the car, on the way from the airport to the conference, that I told her about the problem I had as to where to house my pilgrims."

"With me," the visionary replied, to Lynn's total surprise.

"And I replied, 'With you? You take pilgrims?' And she said yes, they took in pilgrims because they needed the income to live on, just like everybody else in the valley.

"And I was so surprised to find, later, that the home which looks quite large on the outside is almost entirely organised to cater for pilgrims. The entire upstairs rooms are bedrooms, while the whole downstairs is the pilgrims' dining area. On the ground floor, there is a tiny little apartment where Mirjana and her husband and their two children live.

"And she is so wonderful and friendly to everybody. She serves dinner to the pilgrims and sometimes breakfast too, and she will come out and talk with us in the dining-room and answer all the questions that people have. She's wonderful, just like all the other visionaries."

The last years have brought Lynn peace and happiness, which has sustained her during the attacks she has also experienced.

To operate the visits to Medjugorje, she formed a non-profit organisation and neither she nor any of her board members receive salaries for the work they do.

"My husband left me provided for and I pay my way when I come over here, just like the pilgrims. My house is paid for – it's a very small house, but I love it dearly – and my car is paid for, so with the income I have from my husband's death policy, I come here.

"And yes, I have been attacked severely at times by those who would like to say I make a profit from Medjugorje. I have been deeply hurt and upset by these attacks, but I have a very deep gift of faith and I have total belief that what I am doing is from God, because if it were not I don't think I would have the strength to keep doing it.

"At my age, these twice-monthly trips are very difficult and I work hard and long hours at home to try to make each trip as spiritual as possible and to find priests to come with us who will lead us and encourage us. And if it was not all from God, I do not believe that I could continue to do it."

Tomorrow, 2 January 2002, Lynn Hoffman will be sixty-five.

"Most people, when they turn sixty-five," she laughs, "are sitting back and putting their feet up in life. But God's got me busy! I always say to my friends, 'He's working me to death' and they say, 'No, He's working you to life!'"

Many of her pilgrimages bear great fruit.

"On one visit a while back, we had five young men, from their early twenties into their late thirties," she recalls. "It was so wonderful after we got home. One of the young men entered the seminary in Mother Angelica's order and of the other four, three grew greatly in their spiritual lives."

The organisation she has founded is based on spiritual support for priests, many of whom have discovered a deep renewal in their vocations through their contact with Medjugorje.

But the God who called Lynn to this work and the Gospa who watches over her – they have given her a great gift in return.

The heartbreaking pain she initially felt – that her husband had not been able to experience Medjugorje with her – has disappeared.

"After he died, my sorrow was so deep as I travelled without him on the trip we had planned together," she says quietly, a look of serenity coming over her caring face.

"But it was only later, when I was in Medjugorje, that

I understood why it was important that he had not come.

"Because I'm never lonely here. I never miss him here. And that's because he has never been here with me.

"And each time I come to this holy place, the sorrow just melts from my heart and I feel such peace – and yes, even happiness – to know that he is with God and that one day we will most certainly be together again."

"Dear Children," the Gospa said in Medjugorje on 25 August 1990, just days before Lynn Hoffman first set foot in the valley.

"I desire to invite you to take with seriousness and put into practice the messages which I am giving you. You know, little children, that I am with you and I desire to lead you along the same path to heaven, which is beautiful for those who discover it in prayer. Therefore, little children, do not forget that those messages which I am giving you have to be put into your everyday life in order that you might be able to say, 'There, I have taken the messages and tried to live them'. Dear children, I am protecting you before the heavenly Father by my own prayers. Thank you for having responded to my call."

Chapter 14

The reality of God

"My Dear Children," the Queen of Peace said to the villagers of Medjugorje and to the whole world on 25 October 1987.

"Today, I want to call all of you to decide for Paradise. The way is difficult for those who have not decided for God. Dear children, decide and believe that God is offering Himself to you in His fullness. You are invited and you need to answer the call of the Father, who is calling you through me. Pray, because in prayer each one of you will be able to achieve complete love. I am blessing you and I desire to help you so that each one of you might be under my motherly mantle. Thank you for having responded to my call."

The rain that had descended so violently on Bijakovići disappears just as quickly. From outside comes the faint sound of voices, as villagers and pilgrims leave the shelter of houses and doorways to make their way along the narrow winding road.

Through the window of the room in which we sit, a faint ray of sunshine creeps hesitantly. Following its source, I catch a glimpse of a rainbow, high up on the hill of Podbrdo, its shimmering colours fresh and beautiful against the still-grey skies.

Its beauty reminds me of that of the Gospa, as so often described by the Medjugorje visionaries.

"Has Our Lady changed in any way in her appearance over the last twenty years?" I ask Vicka curiously.

The question seems to amuse her and the answer is given with a smile.

"No, she is always the same, from the first time that we saw her. It is only we who have changed and grown older. She remains always the same, full of love and beauty."

Her words remind me of something Fr. Slavko Barbarić wrote in his beautiful book *In the School of Love*:

"The complete beauty of a person cannot be realised without spiritual beauty. For as much as we care for the material and external, so much and no less (if not more) should we care for the spiritual and inner beauty, for the development of the whole person . . . Love of God is that part of the spiritual dress which makes everything valuable and without which all would be empty. Mary was adorned with this kind of dress and for this reason she is the most beautiful of all creatures. She wants all of her children to radiate this same beauty."

It's a beauty that is echoed in the warm smile of Vicka Ivanković, as is so often remarked upon by those who meet with her each day. That, and the sincerity that shines through all she says, as she passes on the messages and the pleas of the Gospa who, for over twenty years, tirelessly continues to call mankind to her Son.

"Prayer, conversion, fasting, peace," Vicka had repeated the Gospa's constant call to yet another group earlier, as despite the threatening rain clouds they packed closely together into the yard, ears straining to catch every word.

"And she requests that every day we pray the joyful, sorrowful and glorious mysteries. Does that seem so much to you? Well then, she says, start slowly but with sincerity, going little by little and step by step forward, every day just a little bit more.

"And she asks us to pray with the heart, not just with our lips.

"Firstly, she says, we should remove all the thoughts that are bothering us and then quietly and honestly, with our hearts, begin to pray until prayer becomes our joy."

On their faces I had seen mixed emotions: curiosity, wonder and a huge hunger to hear how to best respond to this call that comes every day from heaven with such unceasing love.

Just what is it that makes Our Lady especially happy, I ask Vicka, as the rainbow's colours fade then disappear slowly from the sky beyond the net-covered window.

The answer is immediate, simple and exactly what she had said earlier in our conversations.

"Most of all, she is very happy when we accept what she is asking from us. That little by little we start to live her messages and in this way begin to draw closer to the heart of her Son. And her joy is so great for each person who responds to her call in this way."

What is it about us that makes her sad?

"Most of all, it is the separation of families; when we are cursing; when we are not living her messages."

Does she still cry, or show signs of happiness and sadness, as in the early days of the apparitions, I ask?

"I personally never saw Our Lady cry – never! But depending on what she is saying, you can see on her face, just like us, when she is happy or sad."

One more thing, I recall. At the beginning of the apparitions, it was reported that when the Gospa spoke to the six young visionaries she often called them 'My Angels'. How does she address them now?

"Just like she addresses everybody else," Vicka

responds immediately. "She says 'Dear Children' and this is how she calls each one of us who responds to her call, both those who come here to Medjugorje and those others all round the world who hear that call and try to respond to it in their hearts."

As in those very early days on the hillside beyond the window, prayer still remains an integral part of the relationship that has grown and strengthened not only between the visionaries and the Gospa, but also between the Gospa and all those who have, as she asked, responded to her call with their hearts.

Right from the beginning, when they were young and often frightened by the unwanted and threatening attentions of the communist authorities in the region, the visionaries turned for comfort and courage to the Mother of God. She responded by praying and singing with them.

How does she give you courage when you need it now, in these days, I ask Vicka.

"Our Lady has not changed at all," she replies with another warm smile.

"When I need courage, she will pray with me. And as soon as she begins to pray, I feel peace."

Helen O'Gorman stood in the yard of the old house and looked up at the young woman on the steps, just a few feet away.

Her name was Vicka, Helen's husband Ray had just told her. She was one of the six Medjugorje visionaries and all of them came from this tiny village of Bijakovići.

Helen had been dumbfounded at the news.

Coming to Medjugorje had not been her idea of a holiday. In fact, she'd only agreed because it meant so much to Ray to visit this place he'd heard so much about. She, on the other hand, knew practically nothing about it.

Yes, she knew that there were supposed to have been apparitions of Our Lady here – but hadn't that been years and years ago? Something like Lourdes and Fatima? Did the pilgrims not just come here to see the place where these apparitions had supposedly occurred and then go to some holy place and touch a rock or something?

Religion had never played much part in her life up to this – and apparitions even less.

The day's programme had been set to begin with a walk up some mountain or other – Podbrdo they called it. She supposed something had once happened there.

The group had made arrangements to set off early from the house. But she and Ray had been late down to breakfast, only to discover that the others had already left.

Following on a little later, they had walked up a narrow winding road that led through this little village and then on up to the hill behind it.

That's when they'd seen the group of people standing in the yard of an old house with stone steps leading up to a long balcony. Cameras were flashing at a girl who stood on the steps, just a little above the crowd so that all could see and hear her.

Going over to check what all the excitement was about, Ray suddenly stopped in his tracks. "That's Vicka!" he exclaimed. "She's one of the visionaries."

Helen stared at him in amazement.

"Do you mean she's one of these people who have seen Our Lady?" she asked incredulously. "I didn't know they were still alive."

Ray looked at her strangely, as if realising that anything he had said about Medjugorje up to this had gone clean over her head, then quietly began to explain how not only were all the visionaries still alive, but since June 1981 and right up to this day they were still seeing Our Lady, who spoke with them, prayed with them and gave them messages for the world.

"I couldn't believe what he was saying, but moved in closer to see this girl and to hear her," Helen recalls as she sits in her home in Co. Dublin, Ireland, almost twelve years since the morning that was to change so much in her own life.

"She was speaking in her own language and an interpreter was translating for the group, who were mostly Americans.

"And as she talked, something just touched me in my heart.

"I was standing there watching her and I suddenly realised that she was a very very genuine person. I knew by her face! Something just struck me that this girl wasn't pretending about anything. That no matter what else was going on here, this girl was genuine.

"She was so radiant. All the time she spoke, she smiled and I knew that the smile was real. In her face and smile, I could see deep sincerity. And as soon as I realised that, I wanted to hear what she was saying."

Moving in closer to listen carefully, Helen heard the girl reply to a question. Incredibly, she was talking about heaven, hell and purgatory, and how she had seen each one of these places.

It had been All Soul's Day, 1981, when five of the young visionaries (Ivan was absent) had been shown heaven by the Gospa. Records of their experience later told how they had described heaven as 'inexpressibly beautiful' and filled with a multitude of people and angels. Ivanka, it was said, had seen her dead mother there, also another woman from the village.

When they had asked the Virgin why she had shown them heaven, she had replied that it was so that they might see what eternal life would be like for all those who remained faithful to God.

Four days later, it was also recorded, that while the Gospa was with Vicka, Marija and Jakov, she suddenly disappeared and before them they saw hell. It was a terrible sight, they said. Awful, like a sea of flame, in which was a large group of people, all of whom had turned their backs on God.

But that had not been the end of the revelations. Approximately two weeks later, the Gospa appeared to Vicka and Jakov, in Jakov's house. "Praised be Jesus," she said, and told the children that she would take them to heaven.

Jakov began to cry, Vicka said later. He was his mother's only child, he said, so perhaps Vicka should go by herself.

Smiling, the Gospa took Vicka by the right hand and Jakov by the left, standing between them with her face turned towards them. Immediately, they said, they began to feel themselves lifted upwards.

When asked to explain the vision of heaven a few years afterwards, Vicka said it was something that could not be described. Filled with the most beautiful light, flowers, angels and people, and most of all with an indescribable joy, she could only say that a heart would stand still to see it all.

The Gospa had also shown them purgatory, Vicka had said – a much darker place, without the brightness of heaven. Here, the Gospa said, souls were purified before they could enter the heavenly place and much prayer and fasting was required to help them. No sound came from this place, which seemed to have different levels, closer to and further from Heaven, Vicka recalled.

Once more, the Gospa allowed them a glimpse of hell. Vicka did not even want to talk about it, but eventually, when pressed so that a proper record could be kept of the experience, described 'an awful place' filled with flames, a large group of doomed people and ugly creatures that looked like devils.

"I stood there with that American group and listened to this girl Vicka talk about how she had seen heaven, hell and purgatory, and as she spoke I suddenly realised that all of these places existed," says Helen.

"Up to then it had all gone over my head. I had heard, but I had never believed. And now she made them seem so real.

"We stood there and all I could think was – 'My God, there really is a heaven and there really is a hell'. Just the way she talked, I knew that it was all true. Not so much about Medjugorje – I didn't even think of that then – but the whole thing – about faith and how God and Our Lady really existed. That's the thing that touched me deeply.

"Ray was the same. Despite his deep faith, because he had always believed, Ray was in tears as he stood there listening to her. And I remember turning to him and saying, 'But I thought you already knew all that?' And he just replied, 'But I never felt it so real'.

"And that's the way it was. She brought it all to reality for us. She didn't speak to us personally, but later she prayed over everybody, including ourselves. She put her hands on our heads and she prayed, and I felt this firm pressure from her hands.

"She wasn't a stiff, pious person. I remember that while she prayed a decade of the rosary with us, a little child fell and she stopped praying to pick him up.

"And why did I go up to be prayed with? It was simply that she had touched me so much, that I wanted anything that she had. And going back down the hill that day, I was a completely different person."

The experience changed everything, Helen says.

"From there on, everything just blossomed. Before, I'd had no interest in what was going on. We were in a house with all these people and every night they talked about going to Mass and doing the Stations and getting confession and all that. It all just went over my head! I hadn't wanted to know.

"But now it was different. I just wanted to be part of all that was going on – the little prayer group in the house where we were staying and all the religious ceremonies. I felt I had so much time to make up for. Because before now, none of it meant anything to me."

Helen had grown up in Limerick, one of seven children, and had attended a convent school.

"But I didn't have any faith", she says now.

"When I left school, I also left anything to do with religion. I just thought it was all part of the same thing.

"I think I believed in God if I ever thought about it, but to be truthful I didn't really think about it.

"Ray, on the other hand, is a very religious person and always was."

They'd been married for ten years when they went to Medjugorje in June 1990 and right through those years religion and faith meant little or nothing to Helen.

"I'd go to Mass the odd time on a Sunday because of Ray and the kids, but more times than not if I could get out of going I did.

"And that's why it's so surprising that I ever ended up going to a place like Medjugorje!

"Ray works in the ESB and often he would come home and tell me about this place called Medjugorje to which his boss, Gerry Moore, regularly ran trips.

"To me, it all sounded like pie in the sky and I never took any great notice when he tried to tell me about it. I used to think it was all nonsense, but Ray kept on, telling me this and that, how Gerry had been out to Medjugorje again and how such and such a thing had happened. And if anything, it used to annoy me because Ray is so intelligent that I couldn't believe that he could go around listening to all this rubbish at work.

"So one night I just said to him, 'Look, don't tell me about Medjugorje any more. I don't want to hear any more about it – the whole thing sounds ridiculous'. And he took me at my word and for months he never mentioned it again."

One night about six months later, Helen suddenly recalled Ray's interest in this place. "How come you don't talk about it any more?" she asked. "Because you told me not to," he replied.

"So then I found myself asking were things still going on there and he replied yes, that Gerry had been back there recently and such and such a thing had happened. And then he said quietly, 'You know, I'd love to go there'. And that night, just to please him, I said, 'Sure if you want to go, then we'll go'."

She laughs when she recalls the speed with which Ray organised the trip.

"The next day, he went into work and booked the tickets and asked his mother could she take the kids – they were aged seven and four at the time – while we were away, and she agreed. He wasn't giving me a chance to back out, which I would have done!

"That evening he came home beaming and said, 'We're going to Medjugorje on 2nd June'.

"I really didn't want to go and when he brought home a list of things we should take with us, I nearly cried. Candles and a torch and good walking shoes! And all I could think was, here we were with the first chance we'd had since we were married to go away on holiday together. We could have gone anywhere – but we were going to this place called Medjugorje!"

The first few days there didn't mean anything to her, she says.

"We were staying in a lovely house and we had a lovely group and Ray's boss Gerry was the group leader and that was nice. But I was just going along with it all, saying to myself how I'd put up with it for Ray's sake.

"So I went along to Mass with him and didn't voice any criticisms because I didn't want to ruin it for him.

"But it was that experience of seeing and hearing Vicka, three days after we arrived, that changed everything for me. From then on, it was so different and every day was so wonderful."

But would it be different when she returned home? That was the question in Helen's mind at twelve noon as they waited for the coach to pick them up from their house and take them to the airport for the return flight home.

"We were all standing outside the house, waiting for the coach and wondering how we were going to go back home after all that we had experienced here.

"One woman was crying and saying how she didn't want to go home, that it would all be too different to what we'd had here. And I stood there thinking, would I be different back at home? Would I change back to what I had been and forget all this?

"Our house was very close to the big mountain of Križevac and from outside the door we could clearly see both the top of the mountain and the great big cross on its peak. The next minute, the lady of the house came running out to us and said, 'Look up at the cross!' And all ten of us looked up and what we saw was the cross apparently raised up above the mountain. We stared and stared, and kept saying to each other, 'Now, that couldn't be'. And then one old woman in the group said, 'Do you know what it is? There's a cloud between the mountain and the cross. It's just an illusion'.

"We were all happy to believe this, until the next thing we saw the cross going back down onto the mountain top and then back up again!"

Helen is glad, she says, that what was obviously a supernatural sign hadn't occurred earlier in the week.

"If it had happened at the beginning of the pilgrimage, we all decided, we'd probably have been going around looking for signs all week and would have missed what was a wonderful spiritual experience."

And wonderful it had been, she says, since that morning encounter with Vicka and her own sudden realisation of the reality of God.

She attended Mass afterwards with a heart full of joy, she recalls. And she returned to Confession and to the

Eucharist. And the reality of her faith has grown stronger in the years that have followed.

The desire to pray and the peace that comes from this meeting with God is now hugely important to her.

"One of the things that I heard in Medjugorje was to go to your room and pray, and believe that God is listening to you, even if you can't feel that He is.

"I remember going up to my room a few days after we came back and saying, 'Right God, I believe you're listening to me. I can't see you or anything, but I believe you are listening to me. So I'm going to tell you what's worrying me'. And I just talked and talked away, and told Him about particular things that were bothering me at the time. And it was like receiving a personal answer because within a few days solutions came to those problems – things that I wouldn't have thought of myself or been able to do. It was like a confirmation, like He was saying 'Yes, I heard you'.

"And I still feel that way now, twelve years later. My children are now teenagers and my hair has turned grey and when I start worrying about them or anything else, I begin to pray. And I believe that once you pray about something, you leave it there at God's feet and He'll look after it all. You do your best – and leave the rest to Him!

"That's one of the things I most cherish now – being able to talk to God. And being able to try to pass on the faith to my children, so that they won't grow up like I did but will know that it's real and true.

"You see, before I went to Medjugorje, I had no respect for religion or for people who I would have considered 'holy Joes'. I used to joke about people who went to Mass every day. But no sooner had I returned back home than I realised that they were the ones who had the secret all along.

"Medjugorje was a real experience for me. It was only a short week, but it changed everything and the deep feeling I had there of being close to God hasn't left me."

It doesn't mean that everything has gone right and perfect in her life since, she stresses. "A lot of things would have gone wrong, but now nothing gets me down. Even when things go wrong, I have somewhere and somebody to turn to. And that makes a big difference."

She no longer has any fear for death, she says, "even though there have been deaths in the family and sad cases of young people who have died in our community here. But to me, the same sadness isn't there any more when somebody dies.

"You're always going to miss them and, yes, it's sad for the people who are left behind. But not for the person who has died. They're with God!

"That day, you see, when Vicka spoke, I came to the realisation that there really is a heaven and it makes everything here on this earth seem so frivolous in comparison. We worry about so many things – but there's something so much greater there.

"I know now that no matter what happens to any of us, God knows about it. We're not alone – and that's the most important thing of all."

If she hadn't gone to Medjugorje, Helen believes that she would simply have drifted through life. But she feels no great desire to return there.

"Since I've come back, I've never said to anybody – 'You should go there'. It's not about that. What I have said is 'You should pray' or 'You should turn to God for help'.

"And maybe people will read my story and ask – 'Where's the punch-line?'

"Well, the punch-line is that Our Lady called me to

Medjugorje for one reason – so that I would come to know her Son.

"And that's exactly what happened.

"That morning, as I stood outside Vicka's house and looked at her radiant face and her lovely smile – which seemed to me like it must be a reflection of Our Lady's love – something in my heart spoke to me and said, 'You can trust this person'.

"And from that moment I discovered the existence of God.

"Now what I have to do is try to keep on living that faith every day, little by little, in all the ordinary things in my life."

"Dear Children," the Gospa said on 25 June 1990, on the ninth anniversary of her apparitions in Medjugorje and less then three weeks after Helen O'Gorman came to a knowledge of the existence of Mary's Son.

"Today, I desire to thank you for all your sacrifices and for all your prayers. I am blessing you with my special motherly blessing. I invite you all to decide for God, so that from day to day you will discover His will in prayer. I desire, little children, to call all of you to a full conversion so that joy will be in your hearts. I am happy that you are here today in such great numbers. Thank you for having responded to my call."

Chapter 15

Praying for each and every one of you

My time with Vicka is coming to a close.

In just a couple of hours, she leaves Medjugorje for Rome. And when she returns it will be to finalise the arrangements for her wedding to which, it seems, half the world has invited itself.

Several brightly wrapped packages sit on the coffee-table, wedding gifts from friends who had arrived earlier. But whereas most women would be preoccupied with all the fuss of the up-coming marriage, Vicka is – as Mario would say – just Vicka!

Far more interested in the needs of the pilgrims who constantly flock to her door than in worrying about even her own wedding.

Far more concerned with bringing the heartfelt call of the Gospa into the lives of everybody she meets.

In the momentary quiet of the room, I voice the question that has returned constantly to my mind over the last couple of days.

"Do you ever think of the day when Our Lady will no longer appear to you?"

The response comes without hesitation, her warm smile lighting up her face.

"Of course I do.

"I am very thankful for all the days that Our Lady has given us her presence and for so much she has given us – all the graces – but of course I think of those times when she will no longer appear to me every day.

"On the other hand, I could never thank her enough for what she has given me so far.

" And you know," she continues, her head to one side and her smiling eyes challenging me, "we should never put our will in the first place of our lives. Let it always be God's will.

"So, in this way, I can accept the time when I will no longer see her every day because it will be God's decision and Our Lady has always taught us to put God in the first place in our lives and to live the Sacraments in a very real way."

Living the Sacraments is, after all, the essence of everything that is being taught in Medjugorje, in what Fr. Slavko Barbarić called 'the school of love'.

"To live with this Mother," he wrote in his book of the same title, "to be consecrated to her, to be open and devoted to her and, at the same time, to be her student is a great gift and grace.

"Mary, the Mother and the teacher of Christ, wants to be our Mother and teacher. She was the first one to be nourished from the spring of Divine Love when she became the Mother of Love. With love, she wants to lead each of her children to that same spring of love."

But just as Jesus' life and works would be empty without the focal point of His Eucharistic Sacrifice, so the Christian life would be unthinkable without the Eucharist, he continued in the foreword for *Celebrate Mass with Your Heart.*

"The Eucharistic Sacrifice and Christ's presence are proof of his immeasurable love for us," he pointed out.

"Mary, the Mother of Christ, the Mother of the Great Saviour, is the Mother of the Eucharist. She knows what it means for us to be with God in the way He is offered in the Eucharist. For this reason, she invites us to live the Eucharist so that Mass is life, and life is Mass. She invites us to this, and to fasting, so that by living on bread we can discover the true communion bread of God which comes from heaven. For the same reason, she wants us to prepare for Mass so that it can become the focus of our prayers. Our Lady also invites us to adoration of Jesus in the Eucharist, where we are with Jesus, abiding in Him, adoring Him day after day and entering more and more into the mystery of God's presence in the world."

Teaching the young visionaries in her school of love, the Gospa constantly drew them towards the gift of her Son in the Eucharist.

"She has told us that the moments we receive Jesus in the Eucharist are the most important and the holiest moments in our lives," Vicka says, her direct gaze willing me to accept both the seriousness of the message and the great depth of love behind it.

"She says that we should be aware that this is when the living Jesus comes and we receive Him into our hearts.

"That is why she asks that we prepare specially for those moments, so that we become more worthy and can then receive Jesus with all the love in our hearts.

"She asks that our lives should centre around the Mass and the great gift of Jesus in the Eucharist. But she says that before receiving Jesus in the Eucharist, we should prepare our hearts for His coming through prayer and through the Sacrament of Confession."

Vicka's words remind me of something else Fr. Slavko wrote in *Celebrate Mass with Your Heart.*

"This book, along with the others I have written," he said, "bears witness to my experience as a priest in Medjugorje. On the one hand, I have become aware of the inexhaustible spiritual inspiration to be derived from the celebration of the Holy Eucharist, for which I was obliged to prepare personally with prayer and reflection. On the other hand, I also became aware of the danger risked by many priests, lay brothers, sisters and believers when they do not prepare for Mass and Holy Communion, and when they do not give thanks after the Mass. In so doing, they miss completely the meeting with Christ and Holy Mass becomes a duty to be performed every Sunday or even daily."

"Our Lady has also asked", Vicka interrupts my thoughts, "that we read God's word in the Holy Bible every day and that we keep it in a visible place in our homes so as to encourage the entire family to read it and to pray.

"And she has asked for many years now that we renew prayer in our families and in our homes.

"Our Lady promises us that we will be most happy if we bring the prayer of the rosary into our families.

"But most especially, she asks that we should put the Holy Mass in the first place in our lives. That we prepare with our hearts for Jesus in the Holy Eucharist, so that we can then receive Him with our hearts.

"And if we do all of these things, then we are truly responding to her messages, in our lives."

The Gospa's message of 25 October 1996, which I had re-read only last night, comes into my mind.

"Dear Children," she had said to all who would listen. *"Today, I invite you to open yourselves to God the Creator, so that He changes you. Little children, you are dear to me. I love you all and I call you to be closer to me and that your love towards my Immaculate Heart be more fervent. I wish to renew you and lead you with my heart to the heart of Jesus, which still today suffers for you and calls you to conversion and renewal. Through you, I wish to renew the world. Comprehend, little children, that you are today the salt of the earth and the light of the world. Little children, I invite you and I love you and in a special way implore – 'Convert!' Thank you for having responded to my call."*

What is the most important thing that Our Lady says to all those who come to Medjugorje? I ask Vicka, as our last moments together tick away.

"The most important thing is that you listen to Our Lady and that you live her messages with your heart, then return home to transmit this to all those who live around you," she replies with simplicity.

And to those who cannot come?

A warm smile lights up her face.

"It is no different. Our Lady says that she is also close to all those people who cannot come here and that she prays equally for them as well as for all who come.

"It is not who comes to Medjugorje or who does not come that is important. Instead, it is searching for Jesus with the heart and then living with Him in our hearts."

Again, I am reminded of what Vicka had said in one of our earlier conversations about the Gospa.

"She says, 'I look forward to every pilgrim who comes here, but I am most of all happy when you go back to your home and give the messages with joy to others'.

"She says, 'I would be most happy if you received the messages with your heart and every day live them, going forward step by step'."

And that, I realise, encapsulates all that is said and all that is happening here in this valley so specially touched by a Mother's love.

It's time to take my leave.

In just a few minutes, the coach will arrive to take Vicka and Mario to Rome. They are travelling with a returning group of Italian pilgrims and before she goes Vicka has to fetch her suitcase and find her warm coat from under those hanging in the hallway.

Spending this time with her has been enriching, challenging and at times extremely emotional, as the words of the Gospa and her call to the world were repeated to me with sincerity, love and conviction.

For over twenty years, Vicka Ivanković has gazed into the eyes of the Mother of God. For what has seemed like a very short number of hours over an equally short number of days, I in turn have been privileged to study the peace and joy in the eyes and the heart of this visionary.

The experience will always remain in my own heart.

As I thank her and say goodbye, she envelops me in a warm close hug.

Close to tears and reluctant to leave, I find myself asking is there any last, special thing that she would wish to say, about which I didn't ask?

Her answer, given with another hug and a radiant smile, both surprises and touches me deeply.

Because it is a very personal message for you, the reader.

"I would like to greet everybody who will be reading this," she says, a warm beautiful smile transforming her face.

"I wish, for all of you, peace and happiness and that Our Lady will shower you with many blessings.

"I am praying to Our Lady, Queen of Peace, for each and every one of you."

"Dear Children," the Gospa said on 25 February 2002 in Medjugorje.

"In this time of grace, I call you to become friends of Jesus. Pray for peace in your hearts and work for your personal conversion. Little children, only in this way will you be able to become witnesses of peace and of the love of Jesus in the world. Open yourselves to prayer so that prayer becomes a need for you. Be converted, little children, and work so that as many souls as possible may come to know Jesus and His love. I am close to you and I bless you all. Thank you for having responded to my call."